Fun Stuff

Party Cakes

pil

Publications International, Ltd.

Cake illustrations by Shutterstock.

Pictured on the front cover *(clockwise from top left):* Load Up the Dump Truck *(page 40)*, Princess Doll *(page 54)*, Pirate's Bounty Cake *(page 28)* and Underwater View *(page 110)*.
Pictured on the jacket flaps: Tropical Hibiscus *(page 102)* and Gird for the Gridiron *(page 30)*.
Pictured on the back cover *(left to right):* Toy Jeep *(page 32)*, Magical Castle *(page 14)* and Star of the Sea *(page 108)*.

ISBN-13: 978-1-4508-0797-5
ISBN-10: 1-4508-0797-6

Library of Congress Control Number: 2011920270

Manufactured in China.

8 7 6 5 4 3 2 1

Microwave Cooking: Microwave ovens vary in wattage. Use the cooking times as guidelines and check for doneness before adding more time.

Publications International, Ltd.

Contents

How to Make Party Cakes

What's a celebration without the perfect cake as a centerpiece? Once you know the secrets of baking and assembling party cakes, you'll be able to produce an attractive design for any occasion.

Making party cakes can be a simple process if you start with cake mixes and prepared frosting. If you like baking from scratch, feel free to use your favorite layer cake and frosting recipes. Or use our basic recipes for chocolate cake and yellow cake on page 9, which can be baked in pans of different sizes and shapes to suit your needs.

Several recipes, such as Igloo Cake (page 68) and Princess Doll (page 54), call for baking the cake batter in a bowl. Bowl cakes can be made in any ovenproof glass, metal or ceramic bowl; they should be greased and floured just like regular cake pans. (If you use a glass bowl, reduce the oven temperature by 25°F.) A standard cake mix yields about 5½ cups of batter per package, similar to a recipe for any basic two-layer cake. If you have more batter than the recipe requires, pour it into a few

muffin cups lined with paper baking cups. (It never hurts to have a few extra cupcakes on hand!)

Freshly baked cakes can be very tender, making them hard to cut into the exact shapes needed for cut-up cakes. So, it's best to bake your cakes at least one day in advance, let them cool, wrap them tightly and freeze them overnight. Using frozen cakes makes it easier to cut sharp corners and smooth curves without generating lots of crumbs. Giving the cakes an initial light coat of frosting also helps to seal in crumbs and make the final layer of frosting look smooth and professional.

•Bake the Cakes in Advance•

1. Prepare the pans well. You don't want your cakes to stick, so be sure to generously butter and flour your cake pans. Consider lining the bottom of the pans with parchment paper or waxed paper cut to fit the pan. If you prefer, you can use a nonstick pan spray made especially for baking.

2. Preheat your oven to the correct temperature. Mix and bake the cake according to your recipe, or if you're using a cake mix, according to the directions on the package for the cake size you need. Use a spatula to spread the batter all the way into the corners of square or rectangular pans so the top of the cake will be as level as possible. Gently shake or tap the filled cake pans on the counter to level the batter before placing the pans in the oven.

3. Test for doneness. Test to see if the cake is completely baked by inserting a toothpick into the center of the cake; the toothpick should come out clean.

4. Cool thoroughly, then wrap and freeze. Let the baked cakes stand in the cake pans for 10 to 15 minutes after removing them from the oven. Then carefully invert the cakes onto wire cooling racks and allow them to cool completely. If you used parchment paper or waxed paper during baking, you can leave it on the cake layers to help them retain their moisture. Wrap the cooled layers tightly in plastic wrap so they don't dry out. Freeze the wrapped layers until they're firm (at least two hours).

Note: Well-wrapped cakes can remain in the freezer for up to a week; if you want to keep cakes frozen up to a month, store the wrapped cakes in an airtight plastic freezer bag or wrap them in heavy-duty aluminum foil.

Make sure the pan is completely coated to prevent sticking

Allow cakes to cool slightly before turning out onto cooling racks

•Prepare the Cake Board•

1. Buy a cake board. If you don't have a serving tray or cutting board large enough for your cake, purchase standard round and rectangular cake boards at a craft store or a store that sells cake decorating supplies. Standard sizes include 6-, 8-, 10-, 12-, 14- and 16-inch circles, and 14×10-inch and 19×13-inch rectangles.

2. Make your own. If you make a cake that's larger than standard cake boards, cut sturdy cardboard to the size you need. For long, heavy, or unwieldy cakes, consider layering two pieces of cardboard—taping them together with the ridges at right angles—so the board doesn't bend when you lift the cake. You can provide a finished look for such cake boards by covering them with adhesive contact paper. So the edges of the cardboard don't show, cut the contact paper at least 2 inches larger than the cardboard, and fold it over to cover the edges.

3. Wrap the edges or cover the board. If you use two cake boards for strength, wrap the edges with white tape. If you're not using a sanitary base made specifically for holding cakes, wrap the cardboard in aluminum foil or plastic wrap, taping it securely to the bottom with masking tape.

4. Consider a decorative background. If you want an attractive background, cut one set of cake boards the exact same size as the cake. Prepare a larger set of cardboard pieces that you can finish with doilies, gift wrap or other decorative paper. Not only does this provide extra support, but it also allows space for additional decorations around the cake. (You also can create decorative backgrounds with extra frosting or other foods, such as brown sugar, shredded coconut or toasted cake crumbs; apply them after you've finished decorating the cake.)

•Prepare the Decorations•

1. Color the frosting in the shades you'll need. Carefully add a little food coloring to vanilla frosting and blend it in well before adding more. Liquid colors work well, but for more intensity, use paste colors (which can be found at craft or cake decorating supply stores). Keep in mind that most colors will darken a bit after standing, so don't go overboard. Also, dark colors can stain your hands, your counters and your guests' teeth, so be careful when choosing how dark to make your frosting. Mix the colors in bowls that have airtight lids, or cover the bowls with plastic wrap to keep the frosting from forming a crust.

2. Gather any other decorating materials. If a recipe calls for frosting in a piping bag or resealable plastic food storage bag with one corner cut off, get those items ready before beginning so you don't have to stop in the middle of decorating. Also, double check the ingredient list to make sure you have any candies or other decorating supplies you need on hand before you get started.

3. Use a template, if necessary. For complicated diagrams, it may be easier to transfer the design using a template. Make a photocopy of the diagram and blow it up to the same size as the cake. Place a sheet of waxed paper over the cake, then align the diagram with the edges of the cake. Use toothpicks to poke holes around the cutting lines to transfer the markings to the cake.

·Cut & Assemble the Cakes·

1. **Start with well-frozen cakes.** Return them to the freezer or refrigerator between decorating steps to keep them firm for easier decorating.

2. **Mark and cut the cake.** If you've made a template, use it to transfer the design to the cake surface, then remove the diagram and waxed paper. Cut the cake, following the guidelines using a long serrated knife, such as a bread knife. By using a sawing motion, you'll get a clean, straight cut. If your cake has a rounded top, slice it off first to create a flat surface (or use the cake's flat bottom as the decorating surface). Then cut the cakes following the directions for the design you've chosen. To get into tight corners or to cut smooth curves, use a sharp paring knife. Reserve cake scraps for snacking, or crumble, mix with frosting, and use to fill in any gaps or uneven spots in your cut-up cake.

3. **Apply a crumb coat.** Gently brush away loose crumbs with a pastry or basting brush before applying a thin coat of frosting. This seals in crumbs and provides a smooth work surface for the final decorations. Use additional frosting to attach the cake pieces as directed in the recipe. Return the cake to the freezer for 15 to 30 minutes to let the frosting set.

4. **Follow the assembly and frosting instructions for your design.** Carefully transfer crumb-coated cake pieces to your cake board. For added insurance, place a small dab of frosting under the cake pieces to keep them from shifting. For clean decorating, place strips of waxed paper around the bottom of the cake to protect the cake board. Apply the final layer of frosting in the colors called for in the recipe. You may find that an offset spatula makes it easier to apply frosting.

If a purchased frosting seems hard to spread, place it in a microwaveable bowl and heat it on HIGH for 10 to 20 seconds or until it reaches a spreadable consistency, stirring halfway through heating. You can also make prepared frosting more spreadable by beating it with an electric mixer at high speed until it is soft and creamy.

5. **Outline other design elements, if necessary.** Use a toothpick or skewer to trace the decorating design onto the cake surface. Then fill in the areas with contrasting frosting colors, smoothing the frosting as needed to complete your cake.

6. **Apply the finishing touches.** Pipe any additional frosting accents on the cake, then apply candies, cookies, colored sugar or other decorations. Carefully remove any waxed paper strips from around the cake bottom. To remove excess icing from around the cake or on the cake board, use cotton-tipped swabs. To hide any flaws or provide a clean finish to the cake, pipe a frosting border around the bottom of the cake or create a decorative background using cookie crumbs, colored coconut or candies.

Helpful Tools

Serrated knife. The saw blade on a serrated knife allows you to cut frozen cakes with a minimum of tearing or crumbs.

Soft brush. Use a pastry brush to gently clean away stray crumbs after cutting the cake.

Offset palette spatula. The angle of the spatula helps to keep your fingers out of the frosting and allows you to maneuver around curves and corners more easily.

Paring knife. You can use a small paring knife to cut or trim smaller pieces of cake, especially curved pieces.

Decorating tips. Specially shaped metal or plastic tubes can make it easier to add decorative borders, realistic leaves or additional texture to cakes. For example, you can use a star tip to fill in the centers of flowers or to pipe a pretty border.

Piping bag, pastry bag or resealable plastic sandwich bag. For drawing fine lines, writing messages, attaching candies and piping borders or other details, refillable bags allow you to control where the frosting goes and how much you use.

Tweezers. When working with small decorations, using tweezers will help you lift and place them more accurately.

Scissors. If you need to cut taffy, fruit leather or other candies, scissors can help you to cut precise shapes for a variety of decorations.

Basic Chocolate Cake

2 cups all-purpose flour
1¾ cups sugar
¾ cup unsweetened cocoa powder
1½ teaspoons baking soda
1½ teaspoons baking powder
¾ teaspoon salt
1 cup milk or buttermilk
½ cup vegetable or canola oil
2 eggs
1½ teaspoon vanilla extract
1 cup boiling water

1. Preheat oven to 350°F. Grease and flour two 9-inch round cake pans.

2. Combine flour, sugar, cocoa, baking soda, baking powder and salt in large bowl. Add milk, oil, eggs and vanilla; beat with electric mixer at medium speed 2 minutes. Stir in boiling water until well blended. Pour batter evenly into prepared pans.

3. Bake about 25 minutes or until toothpick inserted into centers comes out clean. Cool in pans on wire racks 10 minutes; remove from pans to cool completely on wire racks. Fill and frost as desired.

Makes 12 servings

Note: This batter can also be used to bake a 13×9 cake, bundt cake or cupcakes. For a 13×9 cake, pour batter into a greased and floured pan; bake about 40 minutes. For a bundt cake, pour batter into a greased and floured 12-cup bundt pan; bake about 55 minutes. For cupcakes, line 30 standard (2½-inch) muffin cups with paper baking cups. Fill cups two thirds full with batter; bake about 25 minutes.

Yellow Butter Cake

2 cups all-purpose flour
4 teaspoons baking powder
½ teaspoon salt
1½ cups sugar
½ cup (1 stick) butter, softened
1 cup milk
1 teaspoon vanilla
3 eggs

1. Preheat oven to 350°F. Grease and flour two 9-inch round cake pans or grease and line with waxed paper.

2. Sift flour, baking powder and salt into large bowl. Stir in sugar. Add butter, milk and vanilla; beat with electric mixer at low speed 30 seconds. Beat at medium speed 2 minutes. Add eggs; beat 2 minutes. Pour batter evenly into prepared pans.

3. Bake 35 to 40 minutes or until toothpick inserted into centers comes out clean. Cool in pans on wire racks 10 minutes; remove from pans to cool completely on wire racks. Fill and frost as desired.

Makes 12 servings

Note: This batter can also be used to bake a 13×9 cake, square cakes, bundt cake or cupcakes. For a 13×9 cake, pour batter into a greased and floured pan; bake 35 to 40 minutes. For square cakes, pour batter into two 8-inch square cakes; bake 30 to 35 minutes. For a bundt cake, pour batter into a greased and floured 12-cup bundt pan; bake 45 to 55 minutes. For cupcakes, line 24 standard (2½-inch) muffin cups with paper baking cups. Fill cups evenly with batter; bake 20 to 25 minutes.

Fun & Games

Technicolor Puzzle Pieces

Cakes & Frosting

4 containers (16 ounces each) vanilla frosting

Pink, blue, green and yellow food coloring

2 (13×9-inch) cakes

Decorations & Equipment

2 (20×14-inch) cake boards

Additional rigid cardboard, at least 28×20 inches

3-inch biscuit cutter

Assorted pink, blue, green and yellow candies

1. To prepare cake board, tape boards, side by side, onto additional cardboard with ridges at right angles for better support. Tape edges with white tape or white contact paper. Cover with white contact paper, aluminum foil or decorative paper, if desired; tape securely to bottom of board. Set aside.

2. Tint one container of frosting pink, one blue, one green and one yellow; set aside.

3. Remove cakes from freezer. Trim rounded tops, if necessary, to make cakes level. Mark pieces with toothpick according to diagram on page 114; mark circles with biscuit cutter. Cut frozen cakes using serrated knife and sawing motion for clean cut. Use paring knife to cut out circles.

4. Spread A and B cake pieces with thin layer of pink frosting to seal in crumbs. Repeat with remaining puzzle sections and colored frostings. (Cake may be returned to freezer or refrigerator at this point and decorated later.)

5. Place cake pieces on prepared cake board according to diagram, using frosting to attach sections. Place waxed paper under cake edges to protect cake board. Frost each puzzle piece with colored frosting, using offset spatula to blend contrasting color around cut-out circles to create puzzle pattern. Carefully remove waxed paper from cakes. Decorate with candies.

Makes 24 to 30 servings

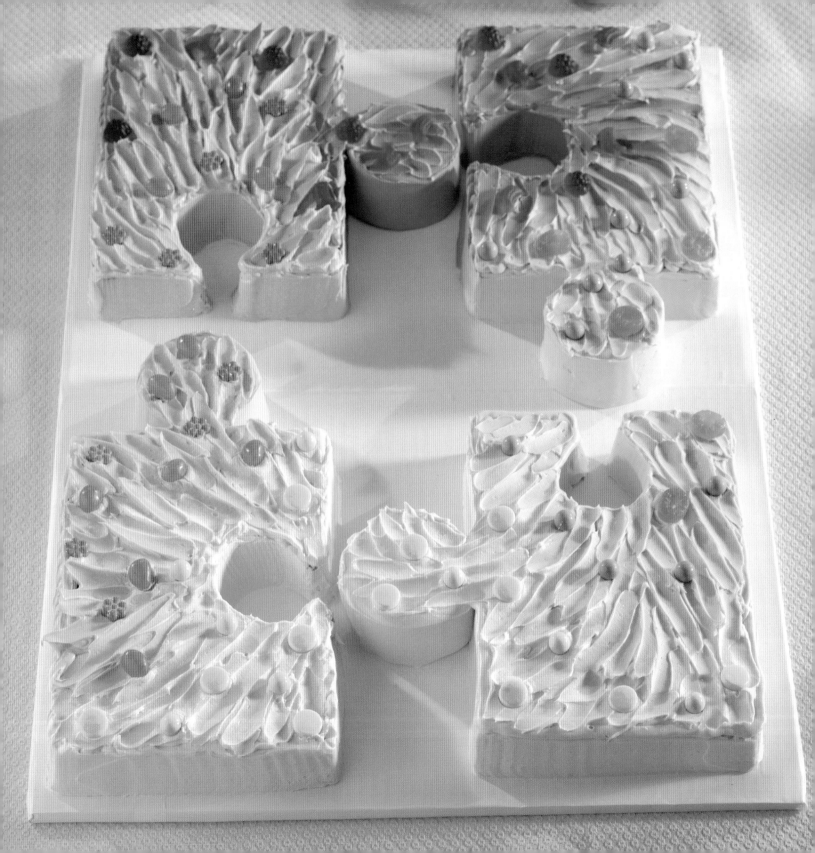

Bowled Away!

Cake & Frosting

2 containers (16 ounces each) vanilla
    frosting, divided
Red food coloring
1 (13×9-inch) cake

Decorations & Equipment

1 (20×14-inch) cake board, cut to
    17×14-inch size to fit cake
Red string licorice
Chocolate-coated mints or mini
    chocolate cookies
Black decorating frosting (optional)

1. Tint half container of frosting red.

2. Remove cake from freezer. Trim rounded top, if necessary, to make cake level. Mark pieces with toothpick according to diagram on page 114. Cut frozen cake using serrated knife and sawing motion for clean cut.

3. Spread frozen cake pieces with thin layer of vanilla frosting to seal in crumbs. (Cake may be returned to freezer or refrigerator at this point and decorated later.)

4. Place cake pieces on prepared cake board, using frosting to attach halves of bowling ball. Place waxed paper under cake edges to protect cake board. Frost bowling pin with vanilla frosting, using offset spatula to smooth frosting. (If desired, place ½ cup frosting in one corner of resealable plastic sandwich bag, cut small tip off bag and pipe outline around bowling pin.)

5. Blend remaining vanilla frosting with red frosting, mixing only enough to create marbled effect. Frost bowling ball with marbled frosting. Carefully remove waxed paper from cake.

6. Arrange licorice on bowling pin for stripes. Add chocolate mints to bowling ball for finger holes. Pipe message on cake board with black frosting, if desired.   *Makes 12 to 16 servings*

Tip: Use a saucer or small plate with a 6-inch diameter to help create the template for the bowling ball.

Magical Castle

Cakes & Frosting

2 containers (16 ounces each) vanilla frosting

Blue food coloring

2 (8- or 9-inch) square cakes

Decorations & Equipment

1 (14×10-inch) cake board or serving platter

4 sugar ice cream cones

4 individual sponge cakes with cream filling

1 flat-bottomed ice cream cone

8 wafer cookies

Assorted gumdrops and small candies

Colored string licorice, cut into strips

1. Tint frosting blue.

2. Remove cakes from freezer. Trim rounded tops, if necessary, to make cakes level.

3. Place one cake on cake board. Place waxed paper under cake edges to protect cake board. Frost cake. Top with second cake; frost top and sides of cake. Carefully remove waxed paper from cake.

4. Place one sugar cone on top of each sponge cake, pushing cake halfway into cone. Frost cones and sponge cakes; press into corners of cake.

5. Frost flat-bottomed cone; place upside-down in center of cake. Press two wafer cookies onto center of each side of cake for castle doors. Decorate cake with gumdrops and candies. Arrange licorice strips to create path into castle.

Makes 12 to 16 servings

Tip

For more vibrant color frosting, use food coloring paste or gels rather than the liquid food coloring commonly available at the supermarket. These pastes and gels can be found at craft and kitchen supply stores, and they are available in a wide variety of colors.

Crayon Craze

Cake & Frosting

2 containers (16 ounces each) vanilla frosting

Gold, green, red, yellow, orange and blue food coloring

1 (13×9-inch) cake

Decorations & Equipment

1 (14×10-inch) cake board

2 flat-bottomed ice cream cones

1. Tint one container of frosting gold. Tint 1 cup of frosting green; place in resealable plastic sandwich bag. Seal bag; set aside. Divide remaining frosting into four small bowls (about ¼ cup each); tint frosting red, yellow, orange and blue. Set aside.

2. Remove cake from freezer. Trim rounded top, if necessary, to make cake level. Mark cake with toothpick according to diagram on page 114. Cut frozen cake using serrated knife and sawing motion for clean cut. Make vertical cut only halfway down to bottom of cake; cut away horizontal section.

3. Spread frozen cake with thin layer of gold frosting to seal in crumbs. (Cake may be returned to freezer or refrigerator at this point and decorated later.)

4. Place cake on prepared cake board. Place waxed paper under cake edges to protect cake board. Frost entire cake with gold frosting, using offset spatula to smooth frosting. Carefully remove waxed paper from cake.

5. Cut small tip off bag of green frosting. Pipe "CRAYONS" on cake (outline letters with toothpick first, if desired). Pipe triangles in bottom corners of crayon box; spread and smooth frosting with offset spatula. Pipe stripes and decorative borders.

6. Carefully cut ice cream cones in half vertically with serrated knife. Frost cone halves with red, yellow, orange and blue frosting. Using small spatula, arrange frosted cones on cake to resemble crayon tips. *Makes 12 to 16 servings*

Good Day to Golf

Cakes & Frosting

3 containers (16 ounces each) vanilla frosting

Green and ivory or yellow food coloring

1 (13×9-inch) cake

1 (15×10-inch) cake baked in jelly-roll pan

Decorations & Equipment

1 cup sweetened flaked coconut

1 (20×14-inch) cake board, cut into 17×13-inch size to fit cake

Sugar wafer cookies

3 to 4 chocolate-covered toffee bars

Chocolate wafer cookies

Chocolate sandwich cookies

1 package chocolate-covered biscuit sticks or 5 (8-inch) wooden skewers

Assorted color gumdrops

1 (6-inch) square matzo cracker

Flat taffy candy

1 (12-inch) wooden skewer

1. Tint one container of frosting green. Tint one container of frosting ivory; place 2 to 3 tablespoons in one corner of resealable plastic sandwich bag. Seal bag; set aside. Place coconut in quart-size plastic bag. Add 1 to 2 drops green food coloring; close bag and shake until coconut is evenly colored.

2. Remove 13×9-inch cake from freezer. Trim rounded top, if necessary, to make cake level. Mark pieces with toothpick according to diagram on page 115. Cut frozen cake using serrated knife and sawing motion for clean cut.

3. Spread frozen cake pieces with thin layer of vanilla frosting to seal in crumbs. Attach pieces A, B and C with frosting; attach pieces D and E with frosting. Place on cookie sheet; return to freezer 10 to 15 minutes or until frosting is set. (Cake may be decorated later.)

4. Place 15×10-inch cake on prepared cake board. Place waxed paper under cake edges to protect cake board. Frost entire cake with green frosting; sprinkle with green coconut. Carefully remove waxed paper from cake. Arrange assembled cake pieces ABC and DE on frosted cake, separating pieces with sugar wafers for floor of cart. Frost both cake pieces with ivory frosting.

5. Place candy bars at front of larger piece for seat. Arrange chocolate wafers for armrests. Cut small tip off bag of ivory frosting; pipe trim along chocolate wafers. Attach sandwich cookies for wheels. For steering wheel, separate one sandwich cookie; scrape filling from one half. Insert biscuit stick into round side of black gumdrop. Attach cleaned cookie half to gumdrop with frosting. Insert into front of cart, pushing biscuit stick through cake.

6. For roof, insert biscuit sticks into round side of four gumdrops; insert into corners of front and back pieces of cart. Pipe frosting onto gumdrops; top with matzo cracker. Arrange gumdrops on front and back of cart for lights.

7. For golf decorations, cut flag from taffy candy and wrap around end of 12-inch skewer for golf flag. Position skewer next to cart. Cut golf bag and clubs from taffy candy with scissors; press together and arrange on back of cart.

Makes 20 to 24 servings

Alphabet Block Cake

Cakes & Frosting

- 2 (8-inch) square cakes
- 1 cup (2 sticks) butter, softened
- ⅓ cup shortening
- 8 cups (2 pounds) powdered sugar, sifted, divided
- ½ cup plus 2 tablespoons milk, divided
- 1 teaspoon vanilla
- Blue and yellow food coloring
- 2½ cups jelly, melted
- Pink decorating frosting

Decorations & Equipment

- 1 (19×14-inch) cake board
- Letter-shaped cookie cutters
- Assorted colored candies
- Colored sprinkles

1. Remove cakes from freezer. Trim rounded tops, if necessary, to make cakes level. Cut each cake horizontally into two layers.

2. Beat butter and shortening in large bowl with electric mixer at medium speed until creamy. Beat in 4 cups powdered sugar, ½ cup milk and vanilla at low speed until smooth. Add remaining 4 cups powdered sugar; beat until light and fluffy. Add more milk, 1 tablespoon at a time, as needed for good spreading consistency. Reserve 3 cups frosting. Tint ¾ cup frosting pastel blue and ¾ cup frosting pastel yellow.

3. Cut cake board into two 7-inch squares; stack and wrap in foil. Cut remaining board into 6½-inch square. Place one cake layer on 7-inch boards; frost top with ¾ cup white frosting. Top with second cake layer; frost top with ¾ cup white frosting. Place 6½-inch board on top of cake; top with third cake layer. Frost top with ¾ cup white frosting. Top with fourth cake layer.

4. Lightly spread jelly over top and sides of cake to seal in crumbs. Frost top and sides of cake with blue, yellow and white frosting, alternating colors. Outline edges of cake with pink decorating frosting.

5. Make outlines on each block using letter cookie cutters. Place remaining frosting in pastry bags with medium writing tip or resealable plastic sandwich bags; pipe outline of each letter. Fill in letters with candies and sprinkles. *Makes 20 to 24 servings*

Tip: Slice and serve top two cake layers first, then remove cake board before slicing bottom cake layers.

Slam Dunk

Cake & Frosting

- 1 container (16 ounces) vanilla frosting
- Orange and black food coloring
- 1 (9-inch) round cake

Decorations & Equipment

- 1 serving platter or 10-inch round cake board
- 3 to 4 black licorice twists
- Small clean sponge

1. Place ¼ cup frosting in one corner of resealable plastic sandwich bag. Tint 1¼ cups frosting deep orange. Tint remaining frosting black; place in one corner of sandwich bag. Seal bags; set aside.

2. Remove cake from freezer. Trim rounded top, if necessary, to make cake level. Place on serving platter. Place waxed paper under cake edges to protect platter.

3. Frost entire cake with orange frosting.

4. Place licorice twists, end to end, around edge of cake to create rim of basketball hoop, trimming licorice as needed. Chill cake 15 minutes to set. Carefully remove waxed paper from cake.

5. Press very slightly dampened clean sponge against top and side of cake to create dimpled surface resembling texture of basketball.

6. Cut small tip off each bag of frosting. Pipe lines on top of cake with black frosting; pipe net design on side of cake with vanilla frosting.

Makes 8 to 12 servings

 *Tip*

When tinting frosting, always start out with a small amount of food coloring, keeping in mind that the color will deepen as it dries. Use a toothpick to add a dab of paste or gel to your frosting, then stir it in completely with a spatula before adding additional color.

Grab That Guitar!

Cakes & Frosting

1 container (16 ounces) chocolate frosting

Brown, black and blue food coloring

3 containers (16 ounces each) vanilla frosting

1 (13×9-inch) cake

1 frozen pound cake (10 ounces), thawed

Decorations & Equipment

1 (24½×16½-inch) full sheet cake board

1 (20×14-inch) cake board

Additional rigid cardboard, at least 31×11 inches

Chocolate-covered wafer cookie

Candy buttons, gumdrops

Black string licorice

1. To prepare cake board, tape boards, end to end, onto additional cardboard with ridges at right angles for better support. Cut to 31×11-inch size. Tape edges with white tape or white contact paper. Cover with white contact paper, aluminum foil or decorative paper, if desired; tape securely to bottom of board.

2. Tint half container of chocolate frosting darker brown with 1 or 2 drops brown and 1 to 2 drops black food coloring. Place 2 to 3 tablespoons in one corner of resealable plastic sandwich bag. Seal bag; set aside. Blend one container of vanilla frosting and 2 to 3 tablespoons chocolate frosting to create tan color. Place ¼ cup tan frosting in one corner of sandwich bag. Seal bag; set aside. Tint ½ cup vanilla frosting blue; set aside.

3. Remove 13×9-inch cake from freezer. Trim rounded top, if necessary, to make cake level. Mark pieces with toothpick according to diagram on page 115. Cut frozen cake using serrated knife and sawing motion for clean cut. Trim top and sides of pound cake to make flat. Cut C and D pieces using serrated knife; save scraps to fill in seam. Spread cake pieces with thin layer of vanilla frosting to seal in crumbs. (Cake may be returned to freezer or refrigerator at this point and decorated later.)

4. Place cake pieces on prepared cake board, using frosting to attach sections. Place waxed paper under cake edges to protect cake board. Frost side of guitar body with chocolate frosting, using offset spatula to smooth frosting. Frost top of guitar body with tan frosting. Mark sound hole on cake with toothpick or edge of glass; fill in with dark chocolate frosting. Frost neck and head with remaining dark chocolate frosting. Outline hand rest below sound hole with toothpick; fill in with blue frosting. Carefully remove waxed paper from cake.

5. Cut small tip off bag of dark chocolate frosting; pipe horizontal lines on neck for frets. Place chocolate wafer cookie about 3 inches below sound hole. Arrange candy buttons between frets and on guitar head; place gumdrops on side of head. Add licorice for guitar strings.

6. Cut small tip off bag of tan frosting; pipe outline around guitar. Pipe additional decorations on guitar body or on cake board, if desired. *Makes 20 to 24 servings*

Tip: To make guitar picks from white and milk chocolate, melt chocolates and spread on waxed paper. Let stand until firm, then use a sharp knife to cut out triangular picks.

Build It with Blocks

Cakes & Frosting

- 4 containers (16 ounces each) vanilla frosting
- Blue and yellow food coloring
- 2 (13×9-inch) cakes*

Decorations & Equipment

- 1 (20×14-inch) cake board, cut to 19×12-inch size to fit cakes
- Mini biscuit cutter (1 to 2 inches)

*For occasions with fewer guests, use one cake and halve the other ingredients.

1. Set aside one container of frosting. Divide remaining frosting in half; tint half of frosting blue and tint half yellow.

2. Remove cakes from freezer. Trim rounded tops, if necessary, to make cakes level. Mark pieces with toothpick according to diagram on page 115. Cut frozen cakes using serrated knife and sawing motion for clean cut. Cut B pieces in half horizontally.

3. Stack A cake layers, spreading vanilla frosting between layers. Spread frozen cakes with thin layer of vanilla frosting to seal in crumbs. (Cake may be returned to freezer or refrigerator at this point and decorated later.)

4. Place layered cakes on prepared cake board; place waxed paper under cake edges to protect cake board. Frost one entire cake with blue frosting, using offset spatula to smooth frosting. Place remaining blue frosting in medium microwavable bowl. Repeat with second cake and yellow frosting, placing remaining yellow frosting in separate microwavable bowl. Carefully remove waxed paper from cake.

5. Use biscuit cutter to cut out 16 cake rounds from B cake pieces. Place 8 cake rounds on wire rack at least 2 inches apart; place sheet of waxed paper under rack.

6. Microwave reserved blue frosting on HIGH 20 to 30 seconds or until frosting reaches pouring consistency. Immediately pour frosting evenly over cake rounds to cover completely; use offset spatula to spread frosting over any bare spots. Let frosting cool. Lift cake rounds from rack with spatula; arrange on cake in rows, using paring knife to push cake off spatula to prevent damage to frosting.

7. Clean wire rack; repeat with remaining 8 cake rounds and yellow frosting.

Makes 24 to 30 servings

Pirate's Bounty Cake

Cakes & Frosting

2 pound cakes (16 ounces each)
1 container (16 ounces) caramel or chocolate frosting

Decorations & Equipment

1 cup chocolate cookie crumbs
1 serving platter or 14×10-inch cake board
15 pretzel sticks, about 3½ inches long
3 mini pretzel twists, 1½ inches wide
1 package small round candies
Assorted candy (ring pops, necklaces, gold coins, etc.)

1. Trim 1 inch from each end of one cake. Cut 1 inch from top of cake to create rectangle.

2. Spread cookie crumbs over serving platter; place cake on cookie crumbs to create cake base.

3. Spread top and sides of cake with frosting, using offset spatula to smooth frosting.

4. Trim 1 inch from each end of remaining cake. Cut long side horizontally in half almost all the way through to create lid of chest. Frost top and sides of cake; place on top of cake base.

5. Raise lid and prop open with pretzel sticks at back and sides. Add pretzel sticks at edges and sides of cake for trim. Push pretzel twists onto front and ends of cake for lock and handles.

6. Decorate lid with small round candies. Fill chest with assorted candy, allowing it to spill out onto platter.

Makes 16 to 20 servings

Tip: Pound cakes are available in both the bakery and frozen sections of the supermarket. Either may be used in party cake recipes, but cutting a pound cake that is partially frozen is easier and generally neater than cutting a bakery pound cake.

Gird for the Gridiron

Cakes & Frosting

2 containers (16 ounces each) vanilla frosting
Green and yellow food coloring
2 (9-inch) round cakes

Decorations & Equipment

1 serving platter or 10- or 12-inch round cake board
Candy wafer

1. Tint one container of frosting green. Place ½ cup vanilla frosting in one corner of resealable plastic sandwich bag. Tint ½ cup frosting yellow; place in one corner of sandwich bag. Seal bags; set aside.

2. Remove cakes from freezer. Trim rounded tops, if necessary, to make cakes level. Mark pieces with toothpick according to diagram on page 116. Cut frozen cakes using serrated knife and sawing motion for clean cut.

3. Spread bottom layer of frozen cake with thin layer of vanilla frosting. Top with remaining cake layer; spread entire cake with thin layer of vanilla frosting to seal in crumbs. (Cake may be returned to freezer or refrigerator at this point and decorated later.)

4. Place cake on prepared cake board. Place waxed paper under cake edges to protect cake board. Frost entire cake with green frosting, using offset spatula to smooth frosting. Carefully remove waxed paper from cake.

5. Cut small tip off bag of yellow frosting; pipe helmet decorations on cake. Cut small tip off bag of vanilla frosting; pipe face guard on helmet. Arrange candy wafer on helmet to resemble ear hole (or pipe circle with vanilla frosting).

Makes 12 to 16 servings

Tip: Choose frosting colors to match your home team.

Road Rally

Toy Jeep

Cake & Frosting

- 1 container (16 ounces) vanilla frosting
  Red and blue food coloring
- ¼ cup chocolate frosting
- 1 frozen pound cake (10 ounces), thawed

Decorations & Equipment

- 1 serving platter or 12-inch round cake board
- 2 individual sponge cakes with cream filling
- ½ graham cracker
  Edible silver dragées
  Black string licorice
- 4 mini chocolate-covered doughnuts
  Sugar-coated gumdrops
  Plain gumdrops
- 2 pretzel rods

1. Reserve ½ cup vanilla frosting. Tint remaining frosting red. Tint ¼ cup reserved frosting light blue. Blend remaining ¼ cup vanilla frosting and chocolate frosting in small bowl to create light brown color.

2. Place cake on serving platter. Trim rounded top, if necessary, to make cake level. Place waxed paper under cake edges to protect platter. Frost top and sides of cake with red frosting. Carefully remove waxed paper from cake.

3. Place sponge cakes, flat sides facing forward, across center and rear of pound cake for seats; frost with light brown frosting.

4. Cut small slit crosswise in front section of pound cake; slide graham cracker half into slit for windshield. Frost graham cracker with blue frosting. Decorate with dragées and licorice.

5. Press doughnuts into sides of cake for wheels; use frosting to attach sugar-coated gumdrops to center of each wheel for hubcaps. Attach plain gumdrops to front and back of cake for headlights and taillights.

6. Cut licorice into four shorter pieces; bend licorice and press into top of sponge cakes for headrests. Cut pretzels into shorter lengths; press onto front and back of cake for bumpers.

Makes 10 servings

Circus Train Mini Cakes

Cakes & Frosting

- 1 package (about 18 ounces) chocolate cake mix
- 1⅓ cups water
- 3 eggs
- ½ cup vegetable oil
- 2 containers (16 ounces each) chocolate frosting

Decorations & Equipment

- Large serving platter or cake board
- 2 round candy wafers
- Candy-coated chocolate pieces
- Licorice snap
- Round candy mints
- Iced animal crackers

1. Preheat oven to 350°F. Spray 6 (4×2-inch) disposable foil mini loaf pans and one disposable foil baking cup with nonstick cooking spray.

2. Beat cake mix, water, eggs and oil in large bowl with electric mixer at low speed 30 seconds. Scrape down side of bowl; beat at medium speed 2 minutes or until well blended. Pour batter into prepared pans, filling two-thirds full.

3. Bake 13 to 15 minutes or until toothpick inserted into centers comes out clean. Remove to wire racks to cool completely. Remove cakes from pans. Trim rounded tops, if necessary, to make cakes level.

4. Position one cake at front edge of platter for engine car. Line up remaining cakes behind engine. Frost cakes, using offset spatula to smooth frosting. Arrange cupcake upside down on top of engine car. Frost cupcake.

5. Place wafers and chocolate pieces on engine car for eyes and mouth and licorice snap for smokestack. Attach mints to each car for wheels. Attach mint to back of last car for taillight. Place animal crackers on tops of cars.

Makes 12 to 16 servings

Big Rig Logging Truck

Cakes & Frosting

1 frozen pound cake (16 ounces), thawed

1 frozen pound cake (10 ounces), thawed

2 containers (16 ounces each) chocolate frosting

8 chocolate sandwich cookies

Candy-coated chocolate pieces

15 pretzel rods

Large gumdrops

Edible silver dragées or sugar pearls

1 candle (7 to 8 inches)

Decorations & Equipment

1 (14×10-inch) cake board, cut to 14×6-inch size to fit cake

1. Trim rounded tops of cakes, if necessary, to make cakes level. Cut 3-inch piece from one end of smaller pound cake (save remaining cake for another use).

2. Spread cake pieces with thin layer of frosting to seal in crumbs.

3. Place cake pieces on cake board according to diagram on page 116, using frosting to attach smaller section to larger cake. Place waxed paper under cake edges to protect cake board. Frost entire cake with frosting, using offset spatula to smooth frosting. Carefully remove waxed paper from cake.

4. Arrange cookies around cake for wheels; attach chocolate piece to center of each cookie with frosting.

5. Break two pretzel rods in half; press into cake edges along sides. Stack remaining pretzel rods on top of cake. Place gumdrops on top of cab and in front and back of truck for lights.

6. Arrange dragées around windshield; press candle into side of cab for exhaust stack.

Makes 12 to 16 servings

Off to the Races!

Cake & Frosting

- 2 containers (16 ounces each) vanilla frosting
- Red and blue food coloring
- 1 (13×9-inch) cake

Decorations & Equipment

- 1 serving platter or 14-inch round cake board
- 4 chocolate sandwich cookies
- Candy-coated chocolate pieces
- 4 chocolate-covered wafer cookies
- Gumdrops

1. Tint one container of frosting red. Place ¼ cup red frosting in one corner of resealable plastic sandwich bag. Tint ¾ cup frosting blue; place in sandwich bag. Seal bags; set aside.

2. Remove cake from freezer. Trim rounded top, if necessary, to make cake level. Mark cake with toothpick according to diagram on page 116. Cut frozen cake using serrated knife and sawing motion for clean cut.

3. Spread frozen cake pieces with thin layer of vanilla frosting to seal in crumbs. (Cake may be returned to freezer or refrigerator at this point and decorated later.)

4. Stand cake pieces on edge on serving platter, using frosting to attach pieces. Place waxed paper under cake edges to protect platter. Frost top part of cake (windshield and windows) with vanilla frosting, using offset spatula to smooth frosting. Frost remaining cake with red frosting. Carefully remove waxed paper from cake.

5. Cut small tip off bag of blue frosting; pipe trim around edges of car, windshield and windows. Pipe numbers, if desired. Press sandwich cookies into sides of cake for wheels; use frosting to attach chocolate piece to center of each wheel for hubcaps. Pipe blue frosting around each hubcap. Cut small tip off bag of red frosting; pipe lines across top of cake for roof accent. Attach chocolate-covered wafer cookies to front and back of cake for bumpers; add gumdrops for headlights.

Makes 12 to 16 servings

Tip: To make sure the cake pieces match on both sides, cut a template from waxed paper in the shape of the car. Place the template on the cake and outline the shape by marking the cutting position with a toothpick. Flip the template over and mark the other side of the cake.

Load Up the Dump Truck

Cake & Frosting

2 containers (16 ounces each) vanilla frosting

Red and yellow food coloring

1 (15×10-inch) cake baked in jelly-roll pan

Decorations & Equipment

10 chocolate sandwich cookies, broken

1 (14×10-inch) cake board

Dark brown sugar (optional)

Candy rocks, round fruit jelly candies

6 mini chocolate-covered doughnuts

Red licorice twists, jelly candy strips

1. Place cookies in food processor; process with on/off pulses until cookies resemble coarse crumbs.

2. Tint one of container frosting red. Tint half container of frosting yellow; place in resealable plastic sandwich bag. Place remaining half container of vanilla frosting in sandwich bag. Seal bags; set aside.

3. Remove cake from freezer. Trim ¼ inch off cake edges using serrated knife and sawing motion for clean cut. Cut cake crosswise into four equal pieces. Cut 3 inches from short end of one piece.

4. Spread frozen cake pieces with thin layer of red frosting to seal in crumbs. (Cake may be returned to freezer or refrigerator at this point, and decorated later.)

5. Place cake pieces on cake board according to diagram on page 117, using frosting to attach sections. Place waxed paper under cake edges to protect cake board. Round front edge of cake with serrated knife. Use toothpick to mark windshield and window areas. Frost cake with red frosting, avoiding window areas and using offset spatula to smooth frosting. Cut small tip off bag of vanilla frosting; pipe windshield and windows. Cut small tip off bag of yellow frosting; outline and fill in frosting on sides and back of truck. Outline doors and grill with yellow frosting. Carefully remove waxed paper from cake.

6. Spread brown sugar around truck, if desired; add candy rocks. Attach jelly candies to front of truck for headlights; press doughnuts into sides of truck for wheels. Arrange licorice and candy strips on top and sides of truck; fill top of truck with cookie crumbs and candy rocks.

Makes 12 to 16 servings

Tip: To make cookie crumbs without a food processor, place the cookie pieces in a resealable plastic food storage bag; run a rolling pin over the bag until the cookies are evenly crushed.

School Daze

Cake & Frosting
- 1 container (16 ounces) vanilla frosting
- Yellow food coloring
- ¾ cup chocolate frosting
- 1 (13×9-inch) cake

Decorations & Equipment
- 1 (19×13-inch) cake board, cut to 15×13-inch size to fit cake
- 2 chocolate sandwich cookies
- Black licorice twists, gummy candies
- Bear-shaped graham crackers
- Assorted color decorating gels (optional)

1. Tint vanilla frosting yellow. Place 2 to 3 tablespoons chocolate frosting in one corner of resealable plastic sandwich bag. Seal bag; set aside.

2. Remove cake from freezer. Trim rounded top, if necessary, to make cake level. Mark cake with toothpick according to diagram on page 117. Cut frozen cake using serrated knife and sawing motion for clean cut.

3. Spread frozen cake with thin layer of yellow frosting to seal in crumbs. (Cake may be returned to freezer or refrigerator at this point and decorated later.)

4. Place cake on cake board. Place waxed paper under cake edges to protect cake board. Frost entire cake with yellow frosting, using offset spatula to smooth frosting. Mark bottom of bus with toothpick; frost with chocolate frosting. Carefully remove waxed paper from cake. Add cookies for wheels.

5. Cut small tip off bag of chocolate frosting; pipe door and windows on bus (outline with toothpick first, if desired). Arrange licorice twists between yellow and chocolate frosting, cutting pieces to fit. Attach gummy candies to front and back of cake for headlights and taillights. Place graham crackers in door and windows.

6. Decorate graham crackers with decorating gels, if desired. Pipe stop sign with decorating gels.

Makes 12 to 16 servings

Tip: For more complex cake diagrams, make a photocopy of the diagram and blow it up to the same size as the cake. Place a sheet of waxed paper over the cake, then place the diagram on the cake. Use toothpicks to poke holes around the cutting lines to transfer the marking to the cake. Remove the diagram and waxed paper, then cut out the cake sections following the guidelines.

Keep On Truckin'

Cake & Frosting
- 2 containers (16 ounces each) vanilla frosting
- Green and yellow food coloring
- 1 (13×9-inch) cake

Decorations & Equipment
- 1 (19×13-inch) cake board, cut to 17×10-inch size to fit cake

- 4 chocolate-covered cookies
- Chocolate cookie or cake crumbs
- Black string licorice
- Yellow and red gumdrops
- Yellow candy wafer

1. Tint one container of frosting green. Place ½ cup green frosting in small bowl; add additional food coloring for slightly darker shade of green. Place in one corner of resealable plastic sandwich bag. Place ½ cup vanilla frosting in one corner of sandwich bag. Tint 2 to 3 tablespoons frosting yellow; place in one corner of sandwich bag. Seal bags; set aside.

2. Remove cake from freezer. Trim rounded top, if necessary, to make cake level. Mark pieces with toothpick according to diagram on page 117. Cut frozen cake using serrated knife and sawing motion for clean cut. Cut rounded triangle from front of piece A to create curved hood as shown in diagram.

3. Spread frozen cake pieces with thin layer of vanilla frosting to seal in crumbs. (Cake may be returned to freezer or refrigerator at this point and decorated later.)

4. Place cake pieces on cake board, using frosting to attach sections. Place waxed paper under cake edges to protect cake board. Use toothpick to mark windshield and window areas. Frost cake with green frosting, avoiding window areas and using offset spatula to smooth frosting. Cut small tip off bag of vanilla frosting; pipe front and back bumper, windshield and windows. Cut small tip off bag of darker green frosting; pipe outline of truck doors and window trim. Outline hood and truck body, if desired. Carefully remove waxed paper from cake.

5. Press cookies into sides of cake for wheels; pipe vanilla frosting in center of each wheel for hubcaps. Place cookie crumbs in cargo area. Pipe trim over wheels and border along bottom of cake with green frosting.

6. Cut licorice; arrange on windshield for wipers and on doors for handles. Add yellow gumdrops for headlights and red gumdrops for taillights. Cut candy wafer in half; attach to doors for side mirrors. Cut tip off bag of yellow frosting; pipe road stripes on cake board.

Makes 12 to 16 servings

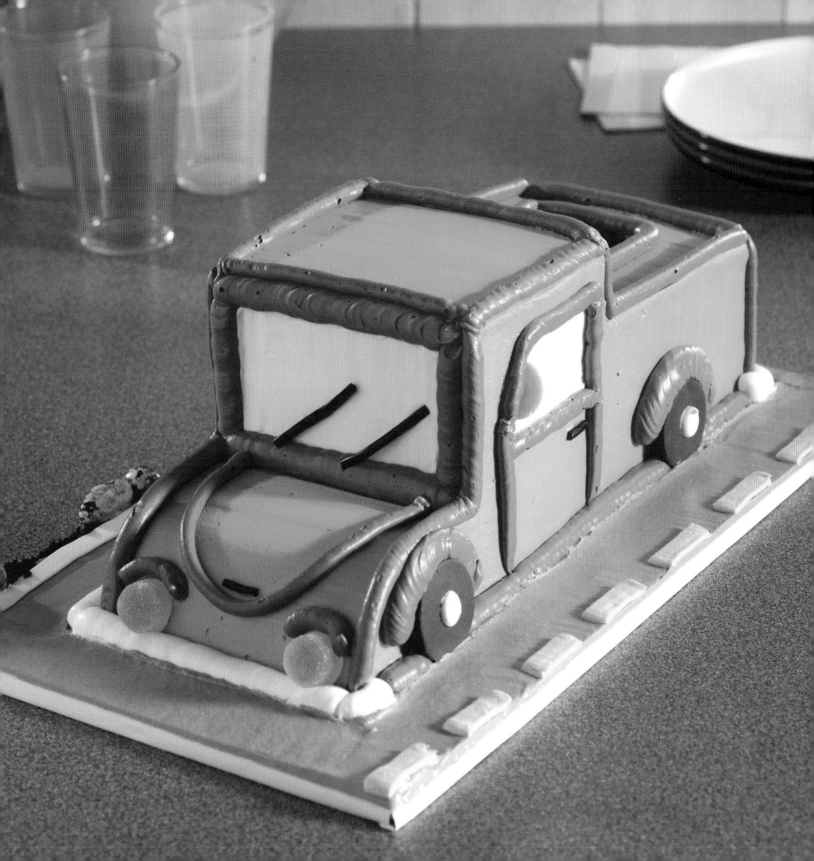

Where's the Fire?

Cake & Frosting

2 containers (16 ounces each) vanilla frosting
Red food coloring
1 (13×9-inch) rectangular cake

Decorations & Equipment

1 (14×10-inch) cake board
6 chocolate and vanilla sandwich cookies
Black licorice twists, red string licorice
Hard candy rings, gumdrops

1. Tint one container of frosting red. Place ½ cup vanilla frosting in one corner of resealable plastic sandwich bag. Seal bag; set aside.

2. Remove cake from freezer. Trim rounded top, if necessary, to make cake level. Mark cake with toothpick according to diagram on page 118. Cut frozen cake using serrated knife and sawing motion for clean cut. Cut triangle from front of piece B to create windshield as shown in diagram.

3. Spread frozen cake pieces with thin layer of vanilla frosting to seal in crumbs. (Cake may be returned to freezer or refrigerator at this point and decorated later.)

4. Place cake pieces on cake board, using frosting to attach sections. Place waxed paper under cake edges to protect cake board. Cut small tip off bag of vanilla frosting; pipe outline of windshield, using offset spatula to fill in and smooth frosting. Frost remaining cake with red frosting. Carefully remove waxed paper from cake.

5. Press cookies into sides of cake for wheels. Arrange black licorice twists along top and bottom of cake. Cut shorter pieces of licorice twists for door handles and ladders.

6. Thread candy rings onto one end of red licorice and arrange on cake for hose. Attach gumdrops to end of licorice for nozzle. Add gumdrops to front, back and top of cake for lights.

Makes 12 to 16 servings

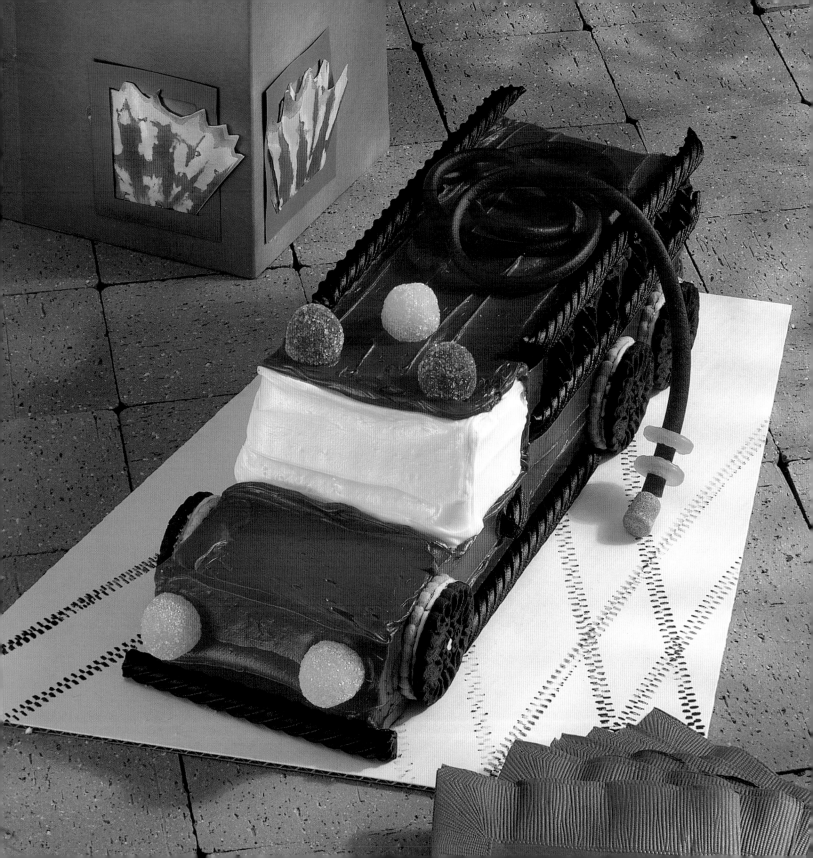

Glamour Girls

Dressing for a Party

Cake & Frosting

2 containers (16 ounces each) vanilla
    frosting
Purple food coloring
1 (13×9-inch) cake

Decorations & Equipment

1 (20×14-inch) cake board, cut to
    17×14-inch size to fit cake
Edible glitter
Black string licorice
White and purple sugar pearls

1. Tint one container of frosting purple. Place ¼ cup purple frosting in small bowl. Add 1 to 2 drops additional food coloring for slightly darker shade; set aside.

2. Remove cake from freezer. Trim rounded top, if necessary, to make cake level. Mark pieces with toothpick according to diagram on page 118. Cut frozen cake using serrated knife and sawing motion for clean cut.

3. Place cake pieces on cake board, using frosting to attach sections. Place waxed paper under cake edges to protect cake board. Spread entire frozen cake with thin layer of vanilla frosting to seal in crumbs. (Cake may be returned to freezer or refrigerator at this point and decorated later.)

4. Frost top of dress with vanilla frosting, using offset spatula to stipple cake surface (hold spatula flat against frosting and gently lift). Frost bottom of dress with purple frosting, using spatula to create swirls along bottom of cake. Use spatula to apply darker purple frosting to create shadows along bottom of dress. Carefully remove waxed paper from cake.

5. Sprinkle top of dress with glitter. Cut licorice into shorter lengths; braid three pieces and press into cake for shoulder straps. Use tweezers to place sugar pearls on waistline of dress; place additional candies at neckline and on skirt as desired. Use additional frosting and candies to decorate cake board with matching "jewelry," if desired.   *Makes 12 to 16 servings*

Tip: If you can't find sugar pearls, substitute white or purple candy wafers or candy-coated chocolate pieces.

Pup in Pink

Cake & Frosting
1 (13×9-inch) cake
2 containers (16 ounces each) milk
    chocolate frosting
½ cup vanilla frosting (optional)

Decorations & Equipment
1 (24½×16½-inch) full sheet cake board,
    cut to 24½×11-inch size to fit cake
Candy wafers, chocolate-covered
    candy mints
Black and red string licorice
Red fruit leather, pink sugar pearls

1. Remove cake from freezer. Trim rounded top, if necessary, to make cake level. Mark pieces with toothpick according to diagram on page 118. Cut frozen cake using serrated knife and sawing motion for clean cut. Cut piece C in half horizontally to make ear; reserve other half to make bone, if desired (see Tip below).

2. Spread frozen cake pieces with thin layer of chocolate frosting to seal in crumbs. (Cake may be returned to freezer or refrigerator at this point and decorated later.)

3. Place cake pieces on prepared cake board, using frosting to attach sections. Place waxed paper under cake edges to protect cake board. Frost entire cake with chocolate frosting; use fork to add texture to frosting, if desired. Carefully remove waxed paper from cake. Place 2 to 3 tablespoons chocolate frosting in resealable plastic sandwich bag. Cut tip off corner of bag; pipe paws on cake.

4. Place white candy wafer on cake for eye; add mints for pupil and nose. Cut small lengths of black licorice; arrange above eye for eyelashes. Use scissors to cut fruit leather into tongue shape; attach to cake. Arrange sugar pearls on cake for collar; add pink candy wafer for tag. Pipe letter on tag with frosting, if desired.

5. For leash, twist or braid lengths of red licorice; insert one end into cake. Attach sugar pearls to leash with frosting, if desired.

Makes 10 to 14 servings

Tip: For bone, frost reserved half of piece C with vanilla frosting. Place remaining frosting in a resealable plastic sandwich bag; cut a large tip off the corner and pipe frosting "knobs" onto each end of the bone.

Accessorize with Rubies!

Cake & Frosting

2 containers (16 ounces each) vanilla frosting

Yellow or gold and red food coloring

1 (9-inch) round cake

Decorations & Equipment

1 (12- or 14-inch) round cake board or serving platter

Red edible glitter, red decorating sugar or red sparkle gel*

Sugar pearls (optional)

*Or use clear edible glitter over vanilla frosting to create a "diamond" ring.

1. Tint one container of frosting yellow. Tint half container of frosting red; set aside.

2. Remove cake from freezer. Trim rounded top, if necessary, to make cake level. Mark pieces with toothpick according to diagram on page 119. Cut frozen cake using serrated knife and sawing motion for clean cut.

3. Spread frozen cake pieces with thin layer of vanilla frosting to seal in crumbs. (Cake may be returned to freezer or refrigerator at this point and decorated later.)

4. Place band section of ring on cake board. Place waxed paper under cake edges to protect cake board. Frost band with yellow frosting, using offset spatula to smooth frosting.

5. Place jewel section of ring on waxed paper. Frost with red frosting; sprinkle with glitter. Lift from waxed paper with spatula and position on cake board as shown in photo. Carefully remove waxed paper from cake. Decorate with sugar pearls, if desired.

Makes 8 to 12 servings

Tip: Edible glitter adds sparkle and shimmer to your cakes without adding any flavor or sweetness. It is available in a wide variety of colors and can be found at craft and kitchen supply stores. Stored in a cool, dry place, edible glitter will keep indefinitely.

Princess Doll

Cakes & Frosting

1 package (about 18 ounces) cake mix, any flavor, plus ingredients to prepare mix

2 containers (16 ounces each) vanilla frosting

Yellow food coloring

Decorations & Equipment

1 serving platter or 10-inch round cake board

1 doll*

Pastel mini marshmallows

Sugar pearls

Small chocolate nonpareil candies

Doll cake picks can be purchased from stores carrying cake decorating supplies, or use doll with legs covered in plastic wrap.

1. Preheat oven to 350°F. Grease and flour 2-quart ovenproof bowl and 8-inch round cake pan.

2. Prepare cake mix according to package directions. Pour 3½ cups batter into prepared bowl; pour remaining batter into prepared pan. Bake cake in bowl 55 to 60 minutes and cake in pan 22 to 28 minutes or until wooden skewer inserted into centers comes out clean. Cool in pans 15 minutes. Loosen edges of cakes; invert onto wire racks to cool completely.

3. Reserve 1 cup vanilla frosting. Tint remaining frosting yellow.

4. Trim flat side of bowl cake and top of round cake to make cakes level. Trim edge of round cake even with bowl cake. Place round cake on serving platter. Place waxed paper under cake edge to protect platter. Frost top of cake with yellow frosting. Place bowl cake, flat side down, on top of frosting.

5. Spread entire cake with thin layer of vanilla frosting to seal in crumbs. Let stand 15 minutes or refrigerate until set.

6. Make small V-shaped hole in center of cake; insert doll in hole. Frost cake and doll torso with remaining yellow frosting. Carefully remove waxed paper from cake.

7. Decorate skirt with flattened marshmallows, sugar pearls and nonpareil candies.

Makes 14 to 18 servings

Tip: To serve, remove doll; slice cake into small wedges.

Pretty Pink Purse

Cake & Frosting

    2 containers (16 ounces) vanilla frosting
      Pink or red food coloring
    1 (13×9-inch) cake
    ½ cup seedless red raspberry jam

Decorations & Equipment

    1 (14×10-inch) cake board
    Black string licorice
    Licorice candies, jelly beans, pastel
      egg sprinkles

1. Tint frosting pink; set aside.

2. Remove cake from freezer. Trim rounded top, if necessary, to make cake level. Mark cake with toothpick according to diagram on page 119. Cut frozen cake using serrated knife and sawing motion for clean cut.

3. Spread frozen cake pieces with thin layer of frosting to seal in crumbs. (Cake may be returned to freezer or refrigerator at this point and decorated later.)

4. Stand cake pieces on edge on cake board from largest to smallest, so cake slopes downward. Use jam to attach sections, pressing gently to adhere. Place waxed paper under cake edges to protect cake board.

5. To make purse shape, measure 1 inch from edge of shortest cake section. Cut off side of cake on an angle, from piece D to piece A. Repeat cut on opposite side of cake. If desired, use cake scraps to fill gaps in top of cake for smooth sloping surface; trim as needed using serrated knife. Spread thin layer of frosting onto cut sides of cake to seal in crumbs. (Cake may be returned to freezer or refrigerator at this point and decorated later.)

6. Frost entire cake, using offset spatula to smooth frosting. Carefully remove waxed paper from cake.

7. Cut 18-inch piece of licorice; gently press into frosting for purse flap. Cut licorice into ½-inch pieces; use tweezers to arrange on edge of cake for stitching. For strap, knot 3 licorice strings together. Braid licorice; knot other end. Push knots into frosting on sides of purse. Decorate purse with candies in flower patterns.

Makes 12 to 16 servings

Touch of Beauty

Cakes & Frosting

- 2 containers (16 ounces each) vanilla frosting
- Purple* and ivory food coloring
- 1 tube black sparkle gel
- 2 (9-inch) round cakes

Decorations & Equipment

- 2 (10- or 12-inch) round cake boards or serving platter
- Edible glitter or granulated sugar
- Oval and round edible silver dragées (optional)

Or use blue and red or rose pink food coloring to create lavender color.

1. To prepare cake boards, cut edge from each cake board to match diagram on page 119; join boards at flat ends. (If desired, tape boards to 24×12-inch cardboard with ridges at right angles for better support). Cover with aluminum foil or decorative paper; tape securely to bottom of board. Set aside.

2. Tint 1 cup frosting lavender. Place one third of lavender frosting in small bowl; add 1 to 2 drops additional food coloring for darker shade. Tint ¾ cup frosting with black sparkle gel to desired "mirror" shade. Tint remaining frosting ivory. Place 1 cup ivory frosting in resealable plastic sandwich bag. Seal bag; set aside.

3. Remove cakes from freezer. Trim rounded tops, if necessary, to make cakes level. Mark cakes with toothpick according to diagram. Cut frozen cakes using serrated knife and sawing motion for clean cut.

4. Spread frozen cakes with thin layer of ivory frosting to seal in crumbs. (Cake may be returned to freezer or refrigerator at this point and decorated later.)

5. Place cakes on cake boards, using frosting to attach cakes. Place waxed paper under cake edges to protect cake boards. Frost top of one cake with "mirror" frosting, leaving ½-inch border. Sprinkle evenly with glitter. Use toothpick to outline two color areas on top of second cake, leaving ½-inch border. Frost with light and dark lavender frostings, using offset spatula to smooth frosting.

6. Frost sides of cakes with ivory frosting, using offset spatula to create swirls. Cut medium tip off bag of ivory frosting; pipe straight line between cakes, curved line between lavender frostings and ½-inch border around entire cake. Add dragées between cakes for hinge and on front of cake for clasp, if desired. Carefully remove waxed paper from cake.

Makes 12 to 16 servings

You Gotta Wear Shades!

Cake & Frosting

2 containers (16 ounces each) vanilla frosting
Red food coloring
1 (13×9-inch) cake

Decorations & Equipment

1 (24½×16½-inch) full sheet cake board, cut to 21×10-inch size to fit cake
Black, silver or green edible glitter
Sugar pearls, edible silver dragées or sprinkles

1. Tint one container of frosting red; set aside.

2. Remove cake from freezer. Trim rounded top, if necessary, to make cake level. Mark pieces with toothpick according to diagram on page 120. Cut frozen cake using serrated knife and sawing motion for clean cut.

3. Spread frozen cake pieces with thin layer of vanilla frosting to seal in crumbs. (Cake may be returned to freezer or refrigerator at this point and decorated later.)

4. Place cake pieces on cake board, using frosting to attach sections. Place remaining vanilla frosting in resealable plastic quart-size bag. Place waxed paper under cake edges to protect cake board.

5. Frost entire cake with red frosting, using offset spatula to smooth frosting. Use toothpick to outline lens area on top of cake; sprinkle with glitter to cover lens area. Use offset spatula to add texture to sunglass frames. (Add additional red frosting to frames, if necessary, to cover glitter that goes outside lens area.) Carefully remove waxed paper from cake.

6. Use tweezers to arrange sugar pearls on sunglass frames. Pipe reflection highlights on lenses with vanilla frosting, if desired.

Makes 10 to 14 servings

Tip: To make sure the cake pieces match on both sides, cut a template from waxed paper in the shape of one side of the frame. Place the template on the cake and outline the shape by marking the cutting position with a toothpick. Flip the template over and mark the other side of the cake.

Ballet Slippers

Cake & Frosting

2 containers (16 ounces each) vanilla
    frosting
Red or pink food coloring
1 (13×9-inch) cake
1 tube pink decorating frosting

Decorations & Equipment

1 serving platter or 14×10-inch
    cake board
Cheesecloth
Pink ribbon

1. Reserve half container of frosting. Tint remaining frosting pink; set aside.

2. Remove cake from freezer. Trim rounded top, if necessary, to make cake level. Cut cake in half lengthwise, then cut each half into ballet slipper shape using serrated knife and sawing motion for clean cut. (Use photo as guide.)

3. Spread frozen cake pieces with thin layer of vanilla frosting to seal in crumbs. (Cake may be returned to freezer or refrigerator at this point and decorated later.)

4. Arrange cake pieces on serving platter. Place waxed paper under cake edges to protect platter. Frost center of each slipper with reserved vanilla frosting, leaving 1 inch on each side and 3 inches at toe and heel.

5. Frost rest of slippers with pink frosting. Carefully remove waxed paper from cake. To add texture, lightly press cheesecloth into frosting and lift off.

6. Outline soles and centers of slippers with pink decorating frosting. Tie ribbon into two bows; arrange bows on toes of ballet slippers before serving. *Makes 12 to 16 servings*

Tip: If you don't have cheesecloth, you can use a slightly dampened clean kitchen sponge or paper towel to add texture to the pink frosting.

Home & Garden

Flutterby Butterfly

Cakes & Frosting

- 1 container (16 ounces) vanilla frosting
- Purple food coloring
- 2 (9-inch) round cakes
- ⅓ cup seedless red raspberry preserves

Decorations & Equipment

- 1 (14×10-inch) cake board, cut to 10×10-inch size to fit cake
- 1 filled rolled wafer cookie
- Gumdrops, gummy hearts, round hard candies

1. Tint frosting light purple; set aside.

2. Remove cakes from freezer. Trim rounded tops, if necessary, to make cakes level. Spread preserves over top of one cake; top with second cake and press lightly to adhere. Cut cake in half crosswise. Cut small triangle from cut side of each half to form butterfly wings as shown in diagram on page 120.

3. Spread frozen cake pieces with thin layer of frosting to seal in crumbs. (Cake may be returned to freezer or refrigerator at this point and decorated later.)

4. Place cake halves on cake board, cut sides facing out, using frosting to attach halves. Place waxed paper under edges to protect cake board. Frost entire cake, using offset spatula to add texture to frosting. Carefully remove waxed paper from cake.

5. Place wafer cookie between cake halves. Decorate wings with assorted candies as desired.

Makes 12 to 16 servings

Dazzling Daisy

Cakes & Frosting

2 containers (16 ounces each) vanilla frosting

Green food coloring

2 (9-inch) round cakes

1 tube yellow decorating frosting, fitted with star tip

Decorations & Equipment

1 (24½×16½-inch) full sheet cake board, cut to 24×11-inch size to fit cake

Chocolate cookie crumbs

Gummy candies (butterflies, worms, bugs)

1. Tint one container of frosting green; set aside.

2. Remove cakes from freezer. Trim rounded tops, if necessary, to make cakes level. Mark pieces with toothpick according to diagram on page 120. Cut frozen cakes using serrated knife and sawing motion for clean cut. Use paring knife to cut between petals.

3. Spread frozen cake pieces with thin layer of vanilla frosting to seal in crumbs. (Cake may be returned to freezer or refrigerator at this point and decorated later.)

4. Arrange all cake pieces except flower center (piece E) on cake board, using frosting to attach sections. Place waxed paper under cake edges to protect cake board.

5. Frost petals with remaining vanilla frosting, using offset spatula to add texture to frosting. Frost stem and leaves with green frosting. Carefully remove waxed paper from cake.

6. Place piece E in center of flower. Pipe yellow frosting with star tip to cover completely. Add cookie crumbs to bottom of cake board for dirt; decorate with gummy candies as desired.

Makes 12 to 16 servings

Igloo Cake

Cake & Frosting

1 package (about 18 ounces) white cake mix, plus ingredients to prepare mix
2 containers (16 ounces each) vanilla frosting
Blue food coloring
1 cup marshmallow creme

Decorations & Equipment

1 serving platter or 10-inch round cake board
1 mini plain cake doughnut
White edible glitter
Rock candy

1. Preheat oven to 350°F. Grease and lightly flour 8-inch ovenproof bowl.

2. Prepare cake mix according to package directions. Pour batter into prepared bowl. Bake 50 to 55 minutes or until wooden skewer inserted into center comes out clean. Cool cake in bowl 10 minutes. Loosen edge of cake; invert onto wire rack and cool completely.

3. Tint ½ cup frosting blue; place in pastry bag fitted with #7 plain tip or resealable plastic sandwich bag with small tip cut from corner. Set aside.

4. Cut cake horizontally into two layers with serrated knife. Spread cake pieces with thin layer of vanilla frosting to seal in crumbs. Place bottom layer on serving platter. Place waxed paper under edges to protect platter.

5. Using long spatula lightly sprayed with nonstick cooking spray, spread marshmallow creme on bottom cake layer to within ½ inch of edge. Place top of cake over marshmallow creme.

6. Attach doughnut to base of cake with vanilla frosting for door. Frost entire cake and doughnut with vanilla frosting.

7. Pipe three circular stripes of blue frosting around cake 2 inches apart. Pipe short, vertical lines between stripes to resemble blocks of ice. Pipe doorway on doughnut. Sprinkle cake with glitter. Break chunks of rock candy; scatter around outside of cake.

Makes 12 to 14 servings

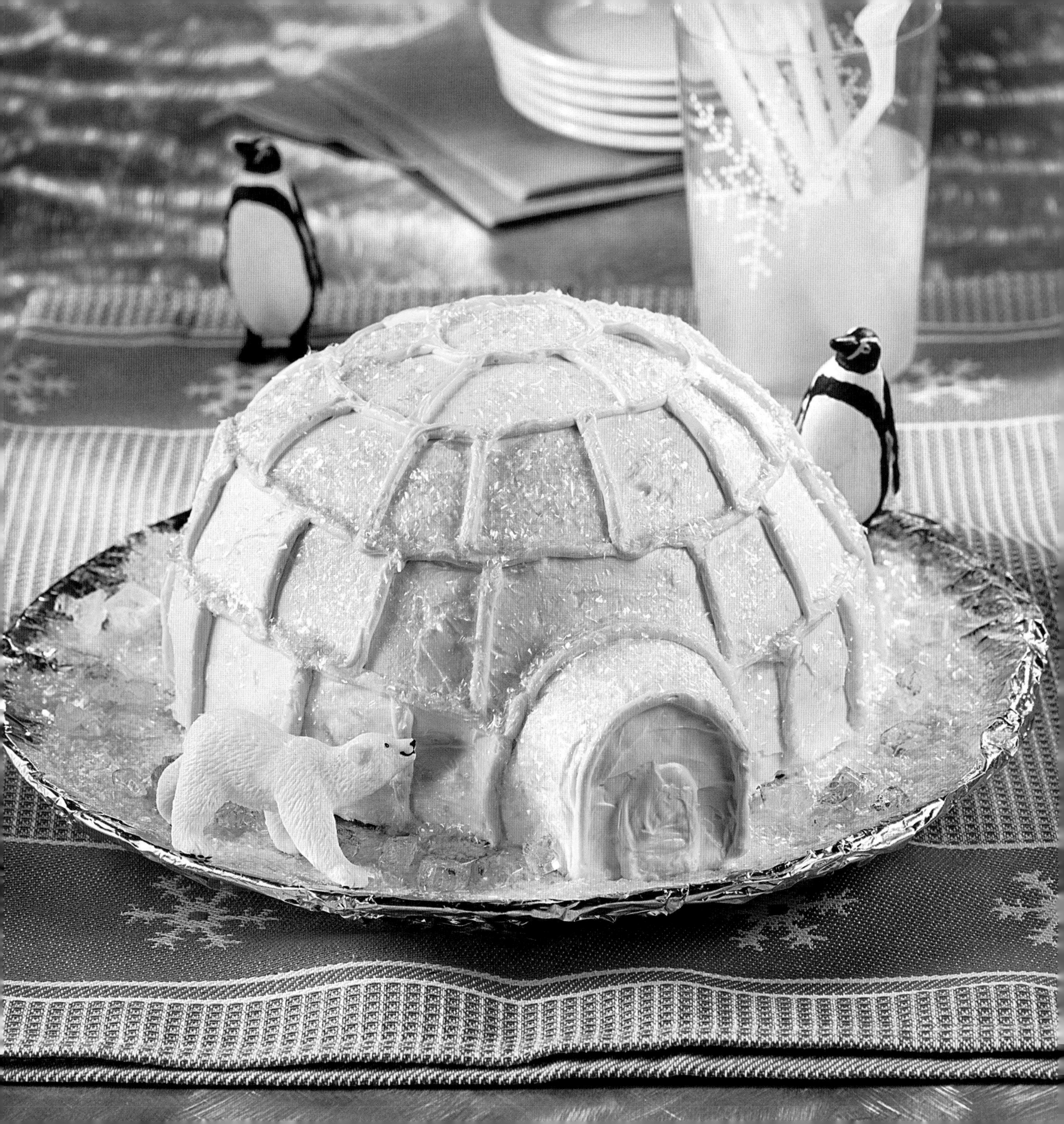

Smiling Snail

Cakes & Frosting

2 containers (12 ounces each) whipped cream cheese frosting

Blue, green, red and yellow food coloring

2 (9-inch) round cakes

⅓ cup seedless red raspberry preserves

Decorations & Equipment

1 serving platter or 19×13-inch cake board, cut to 19×8-inch size to fit cake

Red string licorice, candy-coated chocolate peanuts

10 gingersnaps, crushed (optional)

Candy rocks

1. Tint one container of frosting blue. Tint ½ cup frosting green; place in one corner of sandwich bag. Seal bag; set aside. Tint remaining frosting peach using red and yellow food coloring.

2. Remove cakes from freezer. Trim rounded tops, if necessary, to make cakes level. Spread preserves over top of one cake; top with second cake and press lightly to adhere. Mark top cake with toothpick according to diagram on page 121. Cut frozen cakes using serrated knife and sawing motion for clean cut.

3. Spread frozen cake pieces with thin layer of peach frosting to seal in crumbs. (Cake may be returned to freezer or refrigerator at this point and decorated later.)

4. Stand cake pieces on edge on serving platter, using frosting to attach sections. Place waxed paper under cake edges to protect platter. Frost snail body with blue frosting; frost head and tail with peach frosting, using offset spatula to smooth frosting. Carefully remove waxed paper from cake.

5. Cut small tip off bag of green frosting; pipe spiral on both sides of snail body. Cut licorice into shorter lengths; arrange on snail head for smile and antennae. Add candy-coated chocolate peanuts for eyes.

6. Sprinkle crushed cookies around cake, if desired; garnish with candy rocks.

Makes 12 to 16 servings

Lollipop Garden Bouquet

Cakes & Frosting

2 containers (16 ounces each) vanilla frosting

Green food coloring

1 (8-inch) round cake

1 (9-inch) round cake

Decorations & Equipment

1 serving platter or 10-inch round cake board

½ cup crushed chocolate wafer cookies

Round green hard candies, hard candy rings

Green fruit leather

5 lollipops

1. Tint frosting green; set aside.

2. Remove cakes from freezer. Trim rounded tops, if necessary, to make cakes level. Spread frozen cakes with thin layer of frosting to seal in crumbs. (Cake may be returned to freezer or refrigerator at this point and decorated later.)

3. Place 8-inch cake on serving platter. Place waxed paper under edges to protect platter. Frost top and side of cake, using offset spatula to smooth frosting. Top with 9-inch cake; frost top and side of cake. Carefully remove waxed paper from cake.

4. Sprinkle top of cake with cookie crumbs, leaving 1-inch border around edge of cake. Arrange round candies around top edge of cake. Press candy rings into side of bottom cake.

5. Cut fruit leather into 2½-inch leaf shapes. Press leaves onto lollipop sticks; arrange lollipops in center of cake.

Makes 12 to 16 servings

Home on the Beach

Cakes & Frosting

1 container (16 ounces) vanilla frosting
Green food coloring
4 (9-inch) square cakes
3 containers (16 ounces each) milk chocolate frosting

Decorations & Equipment

1 (19×13-inch) cake board, cut to 12-inch square size to fit cake

Pretzel rods
1 package (15 ounces) large shredded wheat biscuits (3½×2½ inches each)
Shredded wheat crackers
Gummy candy sea animals (fish, sharks, starfish, seahorses)
Hard candy rings, flat taffy candy

1. Tint 3 tablespoons vanilla frosting green. Place in one corner of resealable plastic sandwich bag. Seal bag; set aside.

2. Remove cakes from freezer. Trim rounded tops, if necessary, to make cakes level. Mark pieces with toothpick according to diagram on page 121. Cut frozen cakes using serrated knife and sawing motion for clean cut. Cut piece C in half horizontally for center layer of hut.

3. Spread frozen cake pieces with thin layer of vanilla frosting to seal in crumbs. (Cake may be returned to freezer or refrigerator at this point and decorated later.)

4. Layer square B pieces on cake board with piece C halves in between; spread chocolate frosting between layers and on top of cake. Place waxed paper under cake edges to protect cake board. Attach A pieces with chocolate frosting; place assembled roof on layered cakes. Frost entire cake with chocolate frosting, using offset spatula to smooth frosting. Carefully remove waxed paper from cake.

5. Trim four pretzel rods; press into corners of hut. Cut shredded wheat biscuits in half horizontally with serrated knife. Starting from bottom of roof, attach biscuit halves to roof in horizontal rows, overlapping slightly. Fill in gaps with biscuit shreds.

6. Arrange crackers on hut for door and windows; press into frosting to adhere. Cut small tip off bag of green frosting; pipe grass along bottom of hut. Decorate with assorted candies.

Makes 24 to 30 servings

Summer Sunflower

Cakes & Frosting

3 containers (16 ounces each) vanilla
    frosting
Gold or yellow, green and brown
    food coloring
2 (9-inch) round cakes

Decorations & Equipment

1 (24½×16½-inch) full sheet cake board
Semisweet chocolate chips
Chocolate cookie crumbs

1. Tint one container of frosting gold; set aside. Tint one container green; add 1 to 2 drops of brown food coloring, if desired, for darker leaf color. Tint ½ cup green frosting with additional brown food coloring to make darker shade for center of flower.

2. Remove cakes from freezer. Trim rounded tops, if necessary, to make cakes level. Mark pieces with toothpick according to diagram on page 121. (Use small bowl to mark center circle.) Cut frozen cakes using serrated knife and sawing motion for clean cut; use paring knife to cut out center circle.

3. Spread frozen cake pieces with thin layer of vanilla frosting to seal in crumbs. (Cake may be returned to freezer or refrigerator at this point and decorated later.)

4. Place cake pieces except flower petals on cake board, using frosting to attach leaves to stem. Place waxed paper under cake edges to protect cake board. Frost stem and leaves with green frosting, using offset spatula to add texture to frosting.

5. Frost center circle with brown frosting; top with chocolate chips to resemble seeds. Carefully remove waxed paper from cake.

6. Place petals, one at a time, on waxed paper. Frost each petal with gold frosting. Lift petals from waxed paper with spatula; arrange around center circle in petal shape, using paring knife to push petals off spatula. Garnish bottom of cake board with cookie crumbs.

Makes 12 to 16 servings

Lucy the Ladybug

Cake & Frosting

- 1 package (about 18 ounces) chocolate cake mix, plus ingredients to prepare mix
- 1 container (16 ounces) vanilla frosting
  Red food coloring
- 1 cup chocolate frosting

Decorations & Equipment

- 1 serving platter or 10-inch round cake board
- 12 chocolate discs
- 2 candy-coated chocolate pieces
  Black string licorice
- 1 red ring gummy candy

1. Preheat oven to 350°F. Grease and flour 2-quart ovenproof bowl.

2. Prepare cake mix according to package directions. Pour 4 cups batter into prepared bowl. (Use remaining batter for cupcakes, if desired.) Bake 1 hour and 15 minutes or until wooden skewer inserted into center comes out clean. Cool cake in bowl 15 minutes. Loosen edge of cake; invert onto wire rack to cool completely.

3. Place cake on serving platter. Place waxed paper under cake edge to protect platter. Spread entire cake with thin layer of vanilla frosting to seal in crumbs. Let stand 15 minutes or refrigerate until set.

4. Tint remaining vanilla frosting red. Use toothpick to mark semicircle about 3 inches from edge of cake for ladybug head. Frost remaining cake with red frosting. Place 3 tablespoons chocolate frosting in one corner of resealable plastic sandwich bag. Seal bag; set aside. Frost head with remaining chocolate frosting.

5. Cut small tip off bag of chocolate frosting; pipe line of frosting down center of cake from head to bottom of cake.

6. Press chocolate discs into ladybug body. Press chocolate pieces into center of head for eyes. Cut licorice into short pieces; arrange three pieces above each eye for eyelashes. Cut gummy candy in half for mouth; press into cake.

Makes 14 to 18 servings

Charming Thatched Cottage

Cakes & Frosting

- 2 (8-inch) square cakes
- 2 containers (16 ounces each) vanilla frosting
- 1 tube brown decorating frosting, fitted with plain tip
- 1 tube green decorating frosting, fitted with leaf tip

Decorations & Equipment

- 1 (14×10-inch) cake board
- 1 (10-inch) wooden skewer
- 30 sugar wafer cookies
- Small gummy candies
- Round chocolate-covered cookie

1. Remove cakes from freezer. Trim rounded tops, if necessary, to make cakes level. Mark pieces with toothpick according to diagram on page 122. Cut frozen cakes using serrated knife and sawing motion for clean cut.

2. Spread frozen cake pieces with thin layer of vanilla frosting to seal in crumbs. (Cake may be returned to freezer or refrigerator at this point and decorated later.)

3. Stand pieces A and B on edge on cake board, using frosting to attach sections. Place waxed paper under cake edges to protect cake board. Attach pieces C, D and E with frosting; carefully place on cake base for roof. Push skewer lengthwise through center of chimney piece F, leaving half of skewer exposed at bottom. Attach chimney to roof by gently pushing skewer into cake.

4. Frost entire cake with vanilla frosting, using offset spatula to smooth frosting and create siding effect on front of roof. Carefully remove waxed paper from cake. Frost pieces G, H and I; place next to cottage for window boxes. Use brown frosting to pipe chimney bricks, windows and door.

5. Cut sugar wafers in half crosswise. Starting from bottom edge, press wafer halves into roof in horizontal rows, overlapping slightly. Pipe brown frosting across peak of roof.

6. Use green frosting to pipe shrubbery around cottage and foliage in window boxes. Add candies to window boxes and chimney. Cut chocolate-covered cookie in half; place in front of door for welcome mat.

Makes 12 to 16 servings

Water Your Garden

Cakes & Frosting

2 containers (16 ounces each) vanilla
frosting

Blue food coloring

2 frozen pound cakes (16 ounces each),
thawed

Decorations & Equipment

1 (20×14-inch) cake board, cut to
20×11-inch size to fit cake

Silk flowers or large edible royal icing
flowers

Red candy buttons

Gummy candy butterflies

1. Tint one container of frosting sky blue. Place ¾ cup blue frosting in small bowl; add 1 to 2 drops additional food coloring for darker shade. Place half of darker frosting in one corner of resealable plastic sandwich bag. Seal bag; set aside.

2. Trim rounded tops of cakes, if necessary, to make cakes level. Mark pieces with toothpick according to diagram on page 122. Cut cakes using serrated knife and sawing motion for clean cut. Use paring knife to cut curves in handle. Reserve scraps to fill in seams between cakes.

3. Spread cake pieces with thin layer of vanilla frosting to seal in crumbs. If necessary, fill in seams with cake scraps, attaching with frosting to create level surface. (Cake may be returned to freezer or refrigerator at this point and decorated later.)

4. Place cake pieces on cake board, using frosting to attach sections. Place waxed paper under cake edges to protect cake board. Frost entire cake except top of spout with sky blue frosting, using offset spatula to reach inside of handle. Frost top of spout with darker blue frosting. Carefully remove waxed paper from cake.

5. Cut small tip off bag of darker blue frosting; pipe stripes across watering can and on handle.

6. To protect cake, wrap stems of silk flowers in aluminum foil before inserting into top of cake. Add candy buttons for ladybugs; pipe small dots of darker blue frosting onto candies. Decorate cake board with gummy butterflies.

Makes 20 to 24 servings

Good Eats

Juicy Pineapple

Cakes & Frosting

- 2 containers (16 ounces each) vanilla frosting
- Green, brown and gold or yellow food coloring
- 1 (13×9-inch) cake
- 1 frozen pound cake (16 ounces), thawed

Decorations & Equipment

- 1 (24½×16½-inch) full sheet cake board, cut to 22×12-inch size to fit cake
- Wooden skewers
- Leaf decorating tip

1. Tint one container of frosting green. Place half of green frosting in small bowl; add 1 to 2 drops additional green food coloring and 1 to 2 drops brown food coloring for darker green shade. Tint one container of frosting gold; set aside.

2. Remove 13×9 cake from freezer. Trim rounded top, if necessary, to make cake level. Mark pieces with toothpick according to diagram on page 122. Cut frozen cake using serrated knife and sawing motion for clean cut. Repeat with pound cake.

3. Spread larger cake with thin layer of gold frosting to seal in crumbs; spread pound cake pieces with thin layer of green frosting. (Cakes may be returned to freezer or refrigerator at this point and decorated later.)

4. Place larger cake on prepared cake board. Place waxed paper under cake edges to protect cake board. Frost entire cake with gold frosting, using offset spatula to smooth frosting. Carefully remove waxed paper from cake. Place dabs of light green frosting over cake surface; spread lightly to create marbled effect. Use rounded tip of spatula to create crisscross pattern in frosting.

5. Combine remaining light green frosting and dark green frosting in large bowl, mixing just enough to create marbled effect. Frost sides of pound cake pieces with green frosting. Use skewer to place each cake piece above pineapple; use tip of knife to push cake piece in place.

6. Place remaining marbleized green frosting in pastry bag with leaf tip (or use leaf tip in resealable quart-size plastic bag). Pipe long leaves over top of pound cake pieces.

Makes 20 to 24 servings

Colossal Birthday Cupcake

Cakes & Frosting

1 container (16 ounces) vanilla frosting, divided

¼ cup peanut butter

2 (8-inch) round cakes

Decorations & Equipment

1 serving platter or (10-inch) round cake board

Construction paper or aluminum foil

Fruit-flavored candy wafers

1. Beat ¾ cup frosting and peanut butter in medium bowl until well blended.

2. Trim rounded tops of cakes, if necessary, to make cakes level.

3. Place one cake on serving platter; spread evenly with peanut butter frosting. Top with second cake. Spread top of cake with remaining vanilla frosting, mounding higher in center.

4. Cut 36×3½-inch piece of construction paper; pleat paper every ½ inch. Wrap around side of cake to resemble baking cup. Decorate cake with candy wafers.

Makes 12 to 16 servings

Variations: Substitute chocolate frosting for vanilla, or omit the peanut butter and tint the frosting with food coloring instead. Sprinkle the cake with chocolate shavings instead of candy for an adult party cake.

 *Tip*

For a different look, use heavy-duty aluminum foil instead of construction paper to create the baking cup.

Burger Mania

Cakes & Frosting

9½ **cups cake batter***
1 container (16 ounces) vanilla frosting
1 container (16 ounces) chocolate
    frosting
Red and yellow food coloring

Decorations & Equipment

1 serving platter or 10-inch round
    cake board
12 green gumdrops
1 to 2 tablespoons sunflower seeds

A standard 18-ounce cake mix or two-layer cake recipe will yield about 5½ cups cake batter.

1. Preheat oven to 350°F. Grease and flour 2-quart ovenproof bowl and 2 (8-inch) round cake pans.

2. Pour 4 cups cake batter into prepared bowl; pour 2¾ cups cake batter into each cake pan. Bake cake in bowl 60 to 70 minutes and cakes in pans about 35 minutes or until wooden skewer inserted into centers comes out clean. Cool cakes in pans 15 minutes. Loosen edges; invert onto wire racks and cool completely.

3. Trim flat side of bowl cake and tops of round cakes, if necessary, to make cakes level.

4. Reserve ½ cup vanilla frosting; set aside. Blend ¼ cup chocolate frosting with remaining vanilla frosting to create tan color.

5. Place one round cake on serving platter. Place waxed paper under cake edge to protect platter. Frost top and side of cake with tan frosting. Top with second round cake; frost top and side with chocolate frosting. Top with bowl cake, flat side down; frost with tan frosting. Carefully remove waxed paper from cake.

6. Flatten gumdrops with rolling pin on smooth work surface or sheet of waxed paper sprinkled with sugar. Roll until very thin (about ¹⁄₁₆ inch), turning frequently to coat with sugar. Cut ruffled edge on gumdrops with sharp knife or scissors; tuck underneath burger layer for pickles or lettuce.

7. Divide reserved vanilla frosting in half; tint half red and half yellow. Place each color in pastry bag with medium writing tip or resealable plastic sandwich bag with small tip cut from corner. Pipe frosting around edge of top bun for ketchup and mustard. Sprinkle top of cake with sunflower seeds.

Makes 32 to 36 servings

Pizza Cake

Cake & Frosting

1 package (about 18 ounces) yellow cake mix, plus ingredients to prepare mix
1 container (16 ounces) vanilla frosting
Red food coloring

Decorations & Equipment

1 serving platter or 14-inch round cake board
Orange round gummy candies
Green sugar-coated sour gummy strips, cut into small pieces
Purple round sour gummy rings
White candy-coated licorice strips

1. Preheat oven to 350°F. Grease and flour 12-inch deep-dish pizza pan.

2. Prepare cake mix according to package directions. Pour batter into prepared pan. Bake 18 to 25 minutes or until toothpick inserted into center comes out clean. Cool cake in pan 15 minutes; remove to wire rack to cool completely.

3. Tint frosting red. Place cake on serving platter; frost top of cake to within ¼ inch of edge.

4. Arrange candies over cake to resemble pizza toppings and cheese.

Makes 12 to 16 servings

 *Tip*

Red can be a challenging color of frosting— depending on the type of food coloring used, it often requires more color than you would expect. Since the color darkens with time, it can be helpful to tint the frosting several days in advance to achieve a deep shade of red.

The Chef's Special

Cakes & Frosting
- 1 (9-inch) round cake
- 1 (9-inch) square cake
- 2 containers (16 ounces each) vanilla frosting
- 1 tube black sparkle gel

Decorations & Equipment
- 1 (19×13-inch) cake board
- Silver glitter crystals or edible glitter

1. Remove cakes from freezer. Trim rounded tops, if necessary, to make cakes level. Mark pieces with toothpick according to diagram on page 123. Cut frozen cakes using serrated knife and sawing motion for clean cut.

2. Spread frozen cake pieces with thin layer of vanilla frosting to seal in crumbs. (Cake may be returned to freezer or refrigerator at this point and decorated later.)

3. Place cake pieces on cake board, using frosting to attach sections. Place waxed paper under cake edges to protect cake board. Frost entire cake with vanilla frosting, using offset spatula to add texture to frosting. Carefully remove waxed paper from cake.

4. Use remaining vanilla frosting to add raised billows to top of hat. Outline top and bottom of hat with black sparkle gel. Apply thin line of glitter to create hat band; use additional glitter on top of hat.

Makes 12 to 16 servings

Tip: For a fun presentation, cut the cake board to the same size as the cakes, then assemble the cakes on the board. Trim any cake board edges that show. Wrap a second 19×13-inch cake board with red-and-white checked tissue paper and place the decorated cake on top of the wrapped board.

PB & J Sandwich Cake

Cakes & Frosting

¾ cup powdered sugar

5 tablespoons peanut butter

2 to 3 tablespoons whipping cream or milk

1 tablespoon butter, softened

2 (8-inch) square cakes

½ cup strawberry or grape jam

Decorations & Equipment

1 serving platter or 14×10-inch cake board

1. Beat powdered sugar, peanut butter, 2 tablespoons cream and butter in medium bowl with electric mixer at medium speed until light and creamy. Add remaining 1 tablespoon cream, if necessary, to reach spreading consistency.

2. Trim rounded tops of cakes to remove golden brown layer and make cakes level.

3. Place one cake on serving platter, cut side up. Gently spread peanut butter frosting over top of cake. Spread jam over frosting. Top with second cake layer, cut side up.

4. Cut cake in half diagonally to resemble sandwich. To serve, cut into thin slices across the diagonal.

Makes 12 to 16 servings

Tip

This sandwich cake works well with other sweet fillings (although none are as classic as the PB & J). Try topping the peanut butter frosting with chocolate hazelnut spread or sliced bananas instead of jam. Or spread whipped cream cheese on one cake, then top with sliced fresh strawberries.

Giant Hot Dog

Cakes & Frosting

- 1 frozen pound cake (16 ounces), thawed
- 3 individual sponge cakes with cream filling
- 1 cup chocolate frosting
- 1 tube yellow decorating frosting

Decorations & Equipment

- 1 serving platter or 14×10-inch cake board
- Green gumdrops, chopped

1. Cut ½-inch triangles from corners of pound cake. Use paring knife to round edges of cake to resemble bun.

2. Cut pound cake in half horizontally using serrated knife, cutting almost all the way through but leaving cake halves attached. Place sliced cake on serving platter.

3. Cut ¼ inch off both ends of one sponge cake; arrange in center of bun. Cut ¼ inch off one end of remaining sponge cakes. Place sponge cakes, cut ends together, on either side of center sponge cake to resemble hot dog.

4. Spread chocolate frosting over hot dog, being careful to avoid bun. Pipe yellow frosting on hot dog for mustard. Sprinkle gumdrops over hot dog for relish. *Makes 12 servings*

Tip: To chop gumdrops, first flatten them by rolling them out between two sheets of waxed paper with a rolling pin. Use a sharp knife to cut each gumdrop into narrow strips, then cut the strips crosswise into small pieces.

Flapjack Party Stack

Cakes & Frosting

2 (9-inch) round cakes
1 container (16 ounces) vanilla frosting

Decorations & Equipment

1 serving platter or 10-inch round cake board
1 quart fresh strawberries, hulled and sliced
1 cup caramel or butterscotch ice cream topping

1. Cut each cake in half horizontally using serrated knife.

2. Reserve ¼ cup frosting. Place one cake layer on serving platter; spread or pipe one third of remaining frosting in swirls on cake to resemble whipped butter.

3. Top with sliced strawberries. Repeat with two cake layers, frosting and strawberries. Top stack with remaining cake layer.

4. Microwave caramel topping just until pourable. Drizzle over cake. Pipe or spread reserved frosting in center; garnish with remaining strawberries. *Makes 12 to 16 servings*

 *Tip*

Yellow cakes are the best choice to resemble a pancake stack, but you can give your cakes a little extra pizzazz by adding a few ingredients to the cake batter (homemade or from a mix). Stir in chocolate chips, chopped nuts and/or dried fruit to make these pancakes a sweet sensation!

Seaside Sweets

Ocean Swimmer

Cake & Frosting
- 1 container (16 ounces) vanilla frosting
- Aqua,* blue and yellow food coloring
- 1 (9-inch) round cake

Decorations & Equipment
- 1 (20×14-inch) cake board, cut to 14×12-inch size to fit cake
- Candy wafers, candy buttons
- Graham cracker crumbs or brown sugar (optional)

Or mix green and blue food coloring for desired shade.

1. Tint 1 cup frosting aqua; set aside. Tint ¾ cup frosting blue; place 2 to 3 tablespoons in one corner of resealable plastic sandwich bag. Tint ¾ cup frosting yellow; place 2 to 3 tablespoons in one corner of sandwich bag. Seal bags; set aside.

2. Remove cake from freezer. Trim rounded top, if necessary, to make cake level. Mark pieces with toothpick according to diagram on page 123. Cut frozen cake using serrated knife and sawing motion for clean cut.

3. Spread frozen cake pieces with thin layer of aqua frosting to seal in crumbs. (Cake may be returned to freezer or refrigerator at this point and decorated later.)

4. Place pieces A and B on cake board, using frosting to attach sections. Place waxed paper under cake edges to protect cake board. Use toothpick to mark front and back section of fish body. Frost back of body with blue frosting, using offset spatula to swirl frosting for scales. Frost front of body with aqua frosting; swirl frosting. Frost tail section with yellow frosting.

5. Cut small tip off bag of yellow frosting; pipe fin on top of fish. Cut small tip off bag of blue frosting; pipe mouth. Carefully remove waxed paper from cake.

6. Place piece C on waxed paper. Frost with yellow frosting; swirl blue frosting on top, if desired. Lift from waxed paper with offset spatula; place on cake, using paring knife to push cake off spatula to prevent damage to frosting.

7. Add candy wafer for eye; place candy button in center of eye. Sprinkle graham cracker crumbs over bottom of cake board for sand.

Makes 8 to 12 servings

Tropical Hibiscus

Cakes & Frosting

3 containers (16 ounces each) vanilla frosting

Pink, orange and green food coloring

2 (9-inch) round cakes

Decorations & Equipment

1 (24½×16½-inch) full sheet cake board

Pink, orange and green decorating sugar

Pretzel sticks

Gumdrops

1. Tint one container of frosting pink, one container orange and half container light green; set aside.

2. Remove cakes from freezer. Trim rounded tops, if necessary, to make cakes level. Mark pieces with toothpick according to diagram on page 123. Cut frozen cakes using serrated knife and sawing motion for clean cut (trim additional cake from corners of petals for more rounded look, if desired). Cut two sections in half horizontally; trim with paring knife to make four leaf shapes.

3. Spread frozen cake pieces with thin layer of vanilla frosting to seal in crumbs. (Cake may be returned to freezer or refrigerator at this point and decorated later.)

4. Place petals and leaves, one at a time, on waxed paper. Frost petals and leaves, swirling frosting with offset spatula from edges to centers to create veins. Lift petals from waxed paper with spatula; place on cake board, using paring knife to push petals off spatula. Repeat steps to arrange leaves around flowers.

5. Sprinkle colored sugar down center of petals and leaves. Insert pretzel sticks into gum drops; place in centers of flowers.

Makes 12 to 16 servings

Tip: To create custom colors to match your flower colors, party theme or cake decorations, you can make your own decorating sugar using liquid or paste food coloring. Place granulated sugar in large resealable plastic food storage bags; add 1 to 2 drops of color and shake until the color is distributed. For darker decorating sugars, add additional color, one drop at a time, until the desired shade is reached.

Variations: This cake design lends itself to a number of different flowers. Additional five-petal flowers include pansies, wild roses, buttercups, primroses, violets, petunias and forget-me-nots.

Crabby Crustacean

Cakes & Frosting
- 2 containers (16 ounces each) vanilla frosting
- Red food coloring
- 2 (9-inch) square cakes

Decorations & Equipment
- 2 (24½×16½-inch) full sheet cake boards
- Additional rigid cardboard, at least 29×22 inches
- Hard white candy rings, candy buttons
- 1 package (13½ ounces) graham cracker crumbs or brown sugar
- Gummy sea animals (fish, sharks, starfish, seahorses), foil-covered chocolate coins, candy shells

1. To prepare cake board, tape boards, side by side, onto additional cardboard with ridges at right angles for better support. Cut to 29×22-inch size. Tape edges with white tape or white contact paper. Cover with white contact paper, aluminum foil or decorative paper, if desired; tape securely to bottom of board.

2. Tint one container of frosting red; set aside.

3. Remove cakes from freezer. Trim rounded tops, if necessary, to make cakes level. Mark pieces with toothpick according to diagram on page 124. Cut frozen cakes using serrated knife and sawing motion for clean cut.

4. Spread frozen cake pieces with thin layer of vanilla frosting to seal in crumbs. (Cake may be returned to freezer or refrigerator at this point and decorated later.)

5. Place center cake piece on cake board. Place waxed paper under cake edges to protect cake board. Frost cake with red frosting. Spread small amount of vanilla frosting over cake top, using offset spatula to blend slightly. Use spatula to stipple cake surface (hold spatula flat against frosting and gently lift). Carefully remove waxed paper from cake.

6. Place leg and claw pieces, one at a time, on waxed paper; frost with red frosting. Lift sections from waxed paper with spatula and arrange on cake board around center piece. Add white candy rings for eyes; place candy buttons in centers. Sprinkle graham cracker crumbs around crab for sand. Decorate with additional candies as desired.

Makes 12 to 16 servings

Happy Hula Shirt

Cake & Frosting

2 containers (16 ounces each) vanilla frosting

Turquoise or aqua* food coloring

1 (13×9-inch) cake

Decorations & Equipment

1 (24½×16½-inch) full sheet cake board, cut to 20×16-inch size to fit cake

Candy-coated chocolate pieces

Gummy candy rings and sea animals (fish, sharks, starfish)

Or mix green and blue food coloring for desired shade.

1. Tint one container of frosting turquoise; set aside.

2. Remove cake from freezer. Trim rounded top, if necessary, to make cake level. Mark pieces with toothpick according to diagram on page 124. Cut frozen cake using serrated knife and sawing motion for clean cut. Cut piece D in half horizontally to make two triangles for collar.

3. Spread frozen cake pieces with thin layer of vanilla frosting to seal in crumbs. (Cake may be returned to freezer or refrigerator at this point and decorated later.) Place remaining vanilla frosting in resealable plastic sandwich bag. Seal bag; set aside.

4. Place cake pieces on cake board, using frosting to attach sections. Place waxed paper under cake edges to protect cake board. Frost entire cake with turquoise frosting, using offset spatula to smooth frosting. Carefully remove waxed paper from cake.

5. Cut small tip off bag of vanilla frosting; pipe pocket and shirt seam. Add chocolate pieces for buttons; decorate cake with gummy candies. *Makes 12 to 16 servings*

Variation: Use this basic shirt diagram as a starting point for other designs, such as T-shirts or sports jerseys.

Star of the Sea

Cake & Frosting

2 containers (16 ounces each) vanilla frosting

Orange food coloring

1 (9-inch) square cake

Decorations & Equipment

1 (24½×16½-inch) full sheet cake board, cut to 15×15-inch size to fit cake

Light brown sugar or graham cracker crumbs

Gummy candy seahorses, chocolate shells and starfish

1. Tint one container of frosting orange; set aside. Tint 3 tablespoons of remaining vanilla frosting darker orange. Place in one corner of resealable plastic sandwich bag. Seal bag; set aside.

2. Remove cake from freezer. Trim rounded top, if necessary, to make cake level. Mark pieces with toothpick according to diagram on page 124. Cut frozen cake using serrated knife and sawing motion for clean cut.

3. Turn piece C over so bottom becomes top of cake. Spread frozen cake pieces with thin layer of vanilla frosting to seal in crumbs. (Cake may be returned to freezer or refrigerator at this point and decorated later.) Place remaining vanilla frosting in another sandwich bag. Seal bag; set aside.

4. Place cake pieces on cake board, using frosting to attach sections. Place waxed paper under cake edges to protect cake board. Frost entire cake with lighter orange frosting, using offset spatula to smooth frosting. Carefully remove waxed paper from cake.

5. Cut small tip off bag of darker orange frosting; pipe line down center of each arm. Cut small tip off bag of vanilla frosting; pipe dots of frosting over starfish. Spread brown sugar evenly over cake board for sandy ocean floor. Decorate with additional candies as desired.

Makes 8 to 12 servings

Underwater View

Cakes & Frosting

3 containers (16 ounces each) vanilla frosting

Red, yellow, brown and blue food coloring

2 (9-inch) round cakes

1 cup chocolate frosting

1 tube blue sparkle gel (optional)

Decorations & Equipment

1 (19×13-inch) cake board, cut to 17×12-inch size to fit cake

Candy wafers, chocolate-covered mints

Black string licorice

Gummy candy sea animals (fish, sharks, starfish)

1. Tint one container of vanilla frosting light orange using red and yellow food coloring. Tint ²⁄₃ container of vanilla frosting yellow; place ½ cup yellow frosting in one corner of resealable plastic sandwich bag. Seal bag; set aside. Tint ⅓ container of vanilla frosting ivory using small amount of brown food coloring. Add blue food coloring to half container vanilla frosting; mix just enough for marbled effect. Set frosting aside.

2. Remove cakes from freezer. Trim rounded tops, if necessary, to make cakes level. Mark mask and snorkel pieces with toothpick according to diagram on page 125. Cut frozen cake using serrated knife and sawing motion for clean cut; use paring knife to cut curves.

3. Spread frozen cake and cake pieces with thin layer of vanilla frosting to seal in crumbs. (Cake may be returned to freezer or refrigerator at this point and decorated later.)

4. Place round cake on cake board. Place waxed paper under cake edges to protect cake board. Frost entire cake with light orange frosting, using offset spatula to smooth frosting. Carefully remove waxed paper from cake. Attach mask piece to cake with frosting. Frost top of mask with ivory frosting. Cut tip off bag of yellow frosting; pipe border around mask.

5. Place snorkel pieces, one at a time, on waxed paper. Frost with yellow frosting. Lift sections from waxed paper with spatula and position on cake board. Use offset spatula to smooth frosting and hide seams.

6. Place chocolate frosting in one corner of sandwich bag. Cut small tip off bag; pipe spikes of frosting for hair. Add candy wafers for eyes and cheeks; place chocolate mint in center of each eye. Add licorice for smile.

7. Use offset spatula to cover cake board with marbleized frosting, swirling for wave effect. Outline waves with blue sparkle gel, if desired. Decorate with gummy candies as desired.

Makes 12 to 16 servings

Gone Fishin'

Cake & Frosting

- 3 containers (16 ounces each) vanilla frosting
- Green, blue and orange food coloring
- 1 (13×9-inch) cake
- 1 container (16 ounces) chocolate frosting
- 2 chocolate-coated cake rolls

Decorations & Equipment

- 1 (24½×16½-inch) full sheet cake board
- Candy wafers, hard candy rings, candy dots
- Black string licorice
- Chocolate cookie crumbs (optional)
- Gummy worms (optional)

1. Tint half container of vanilla frosting green, half container blue and half container orange. Place 1 to 2 tablespoons of each color in corners of three separate resealable plastic sandwich bags. Seal bags; set aside.

2. Remove cake from freezer. Trim rounded top, if necessary, to make cake level. Mark pieces with toothpick according to diagram on page 125. Cut frozen cake using serrated knife and sawing motion for clean cut; use paring knife to cut curves.

3. Spread frozen cake pieces with thin layer of vanilla frosting to seal in crumbs. (Cake may be returned to freezer or refrigerator at this point and decorated later.)

4. Place pole pieces, one at a time, on waxed paper. Frost with chocolate frosting, using offset spatula to smooth frosting. Lift cake from waxed paper with spatula; place on prepared cake board, curving cake as necessary to fit. Smooth frosting at seams. Press candy rings into pole; thread licorice through rings, extending licorice beyond pole. Cut cake rolls in half and attach to bottom of pole with chocolate frosting.

5. Place fish pieces on waxed paper. Frost with colored frostings, using offset spatula to ruffle fish tails. Lift fish from waxed paper with wide spatula. Arrange on cake board, using paring knife to push cake off spatula to prevent damage to frosting.

6. Add candy wafers for fish scales and candies for eyes. Cut small tips off bags of colored frosting. Pipe mouths on fish, using contrasting colors. Run licorice pieces from mouths of fish to top of fishing pole. Pipe water accents on cake board with blue frosting. Add bowl of cookie crumbs and gummy worms, if desired. *Makes 12 to 16 servings*

Technicolor Puzzle Pieces · Page 10

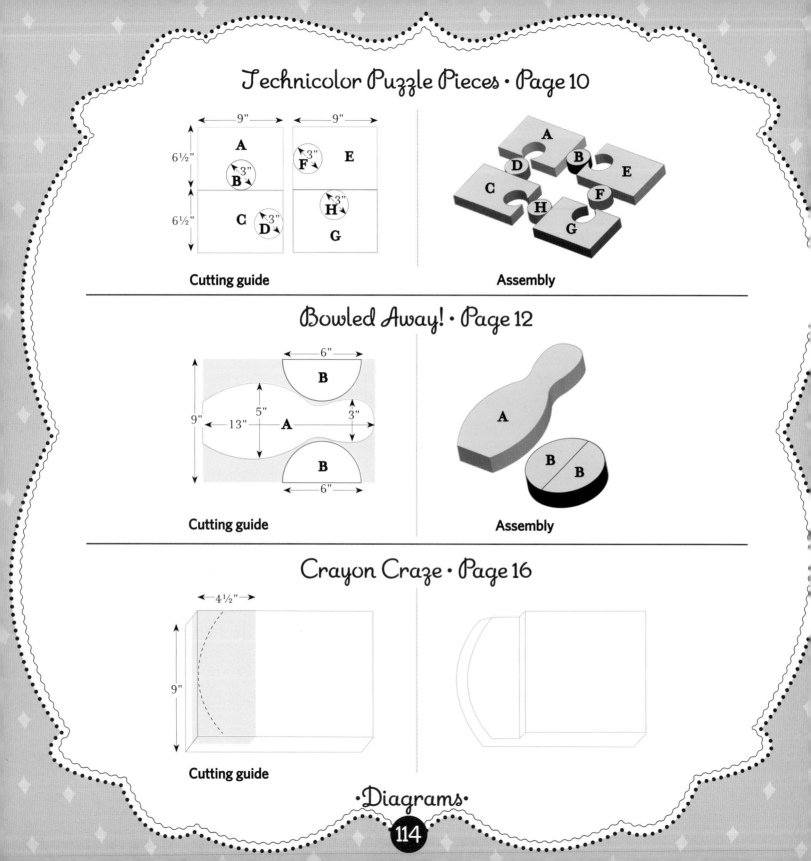

Cutting guide

Assembly

Bowled Away! · Page 12

Cutting guide

Assembly

Crayon Craze · Page 16

Cutting guide

Good Day to Golf · Page 18

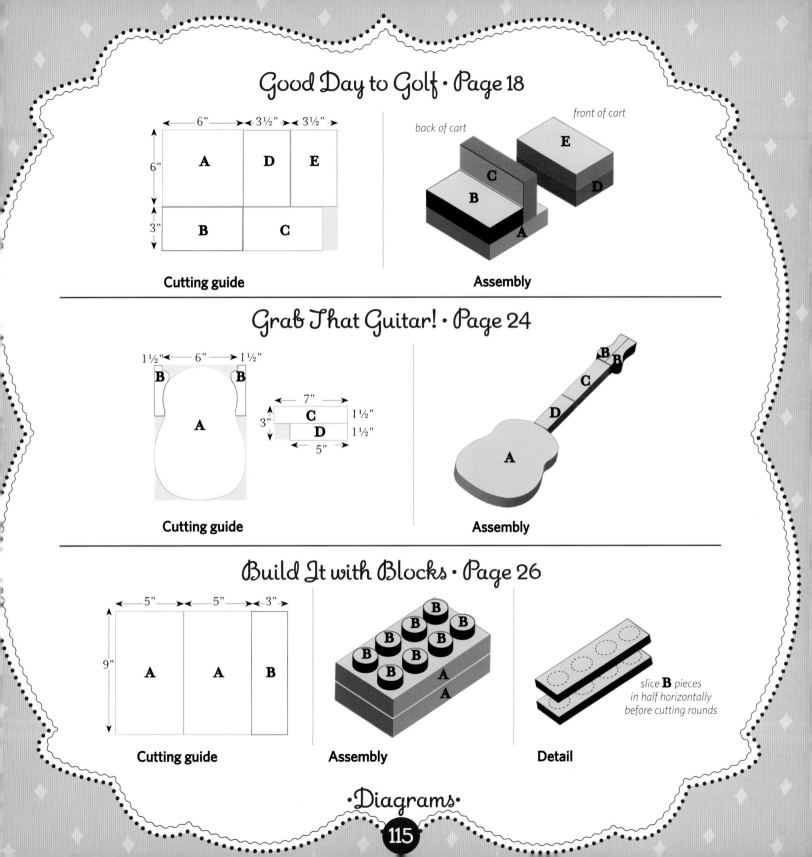

6" | **3½"** | **3½"**

6" A | D | E

3" B | C

Cutting guide

back of cart

front of cart

E
C
B
D
A

Assembly

Grab That Guitar! · Page 24

1½" | **6"** | 1½"

B | | B

A

7"

3" C | 1½"
D | 1½"

5"

Cutting guide

B B
C
D
A

Assembly

Build It with Blocks · Page 26

5" | **5"** | **3"**

9" A | A | B

Cutting guide

B B B B
B B B B
B
A
A

Assembly

slice **B** pieces
in half horizontally
before cutting rounds

Detail

Gird for the Gridiron · Page 30

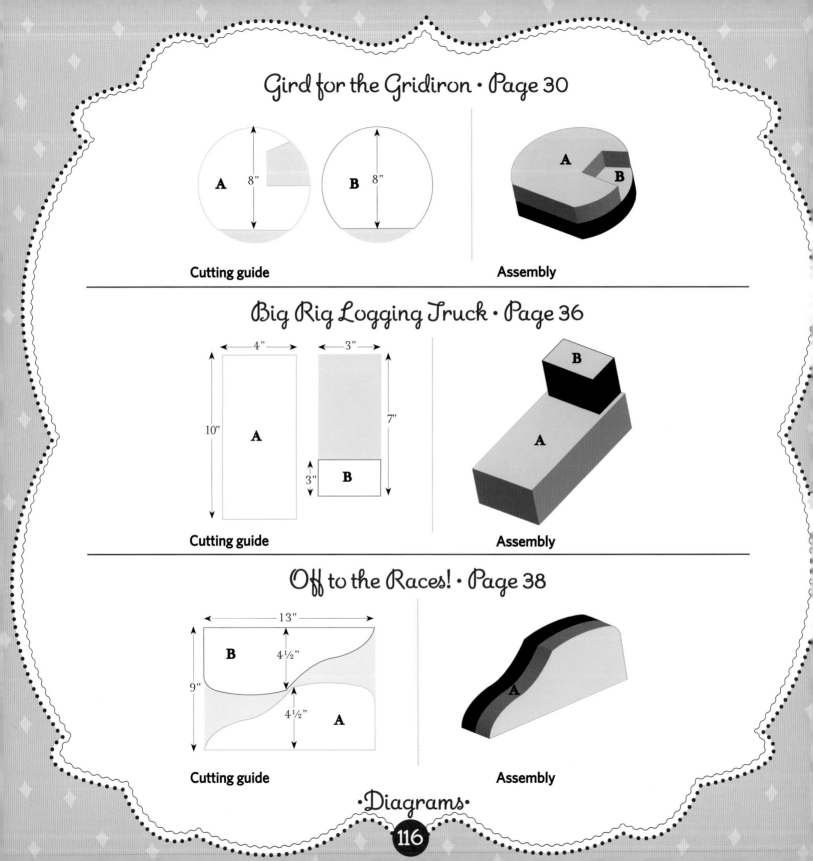

A 8" B 8"

Cutting guide

A B

Assembly

Big Rig Logging Truck · Page 36

4" 3"

10" A 7"

3" B

Cutting guide

B A

Assembly

Off to the Races! · Page 38

13"

B 4½"

9" 4½" A

Cutting guide

A

Assembly

Load Up the Dump Truck · Page 40

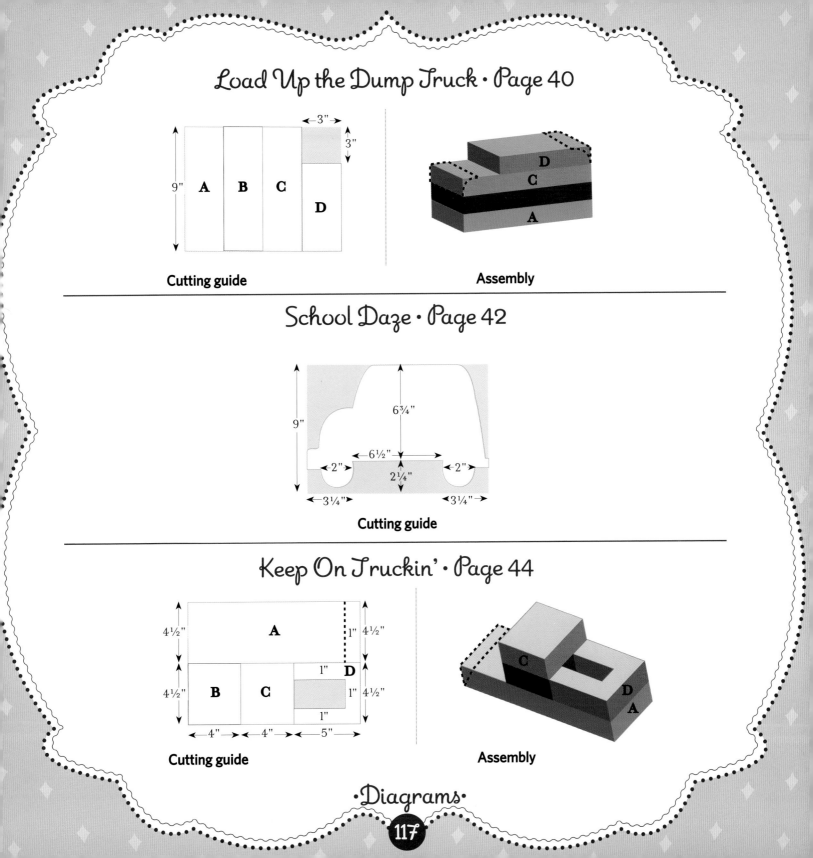

Cutting guide

Assembly

A B C D

9"

3"

3"

D
C
A

School Daze · Page 42

9"

6¾"

6½"

2¼"

2"   2"

3¼"   3¼"

Cutting guide

Keep On Truckin' · Page 44

A

B   C   D

4½"   4½"

4½"   4½"

1"

1"

1"

1"

4"   4"   5"

Cutting guide

Assembly

C

D
A

Where's the Fire? · Page 46

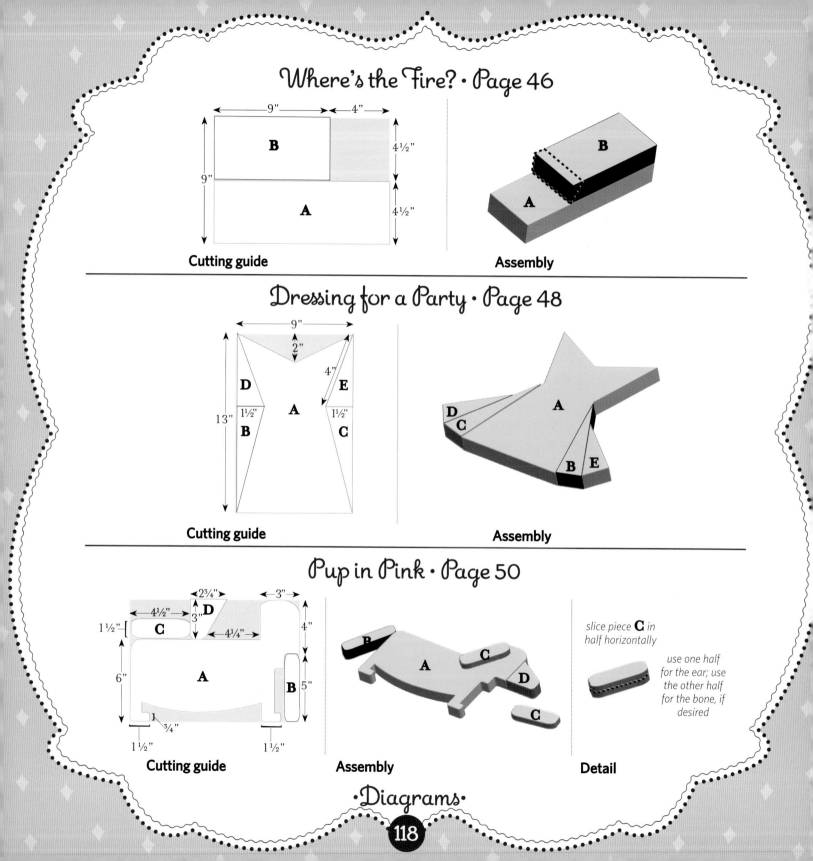

9" 4"

9" 4½" 4½"

B

A

B

A

Cutting guide

Assembly

Dressing for a Party · Page 48

9"

2"

4"

D **E**

1½" 1½"

13" **A**

B **C**

A

D
C

B **E**

Cutting guide

Assembly

Pup in Pink · Page 50

2¾" 3"

4½" **D**

1½" **C** 3"

4¼" 4"

6" **A** **B** 5"

1 ¾"

1½" 1½"

B

A **C**

D

C

*slice piece **C** in half horizontally*

use one half for the ear; use the other half for the bone, if desired

Cutting guide

Assembly

Detail

·Diagrams·

Accessorize with Rubies! · Page 52

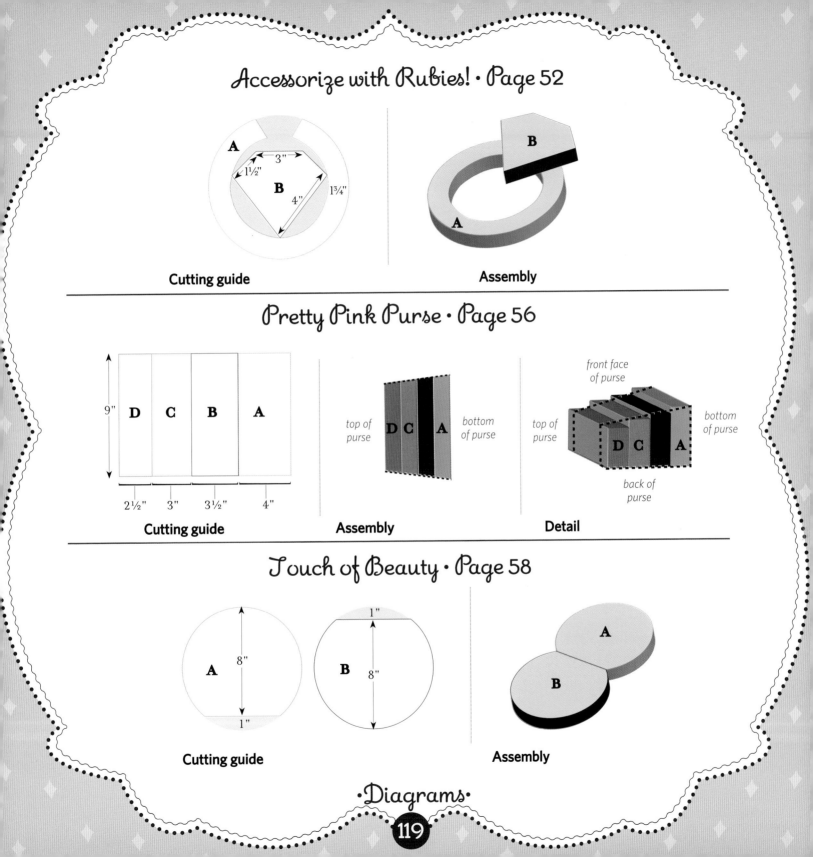

A

3"

1½"

B

4"

1¾"

Cutting guide

B

A

Assembly

Pretty Pink Purse · Page 56

9"

D **C** **B** **A**

2½" 3" 3½" 4"

Cutting guide

top of purse

D C **A**

bottom of purse

Assembly

front face of purse

top of purse

D C **A**

bottom of purse

back of purse

Detail

Touch of Beauty · Page 58

A

8"

1"

1"

B

8"

Cutting guide

A

B

Assembly

You Gotta Wear Shades! · Page 60

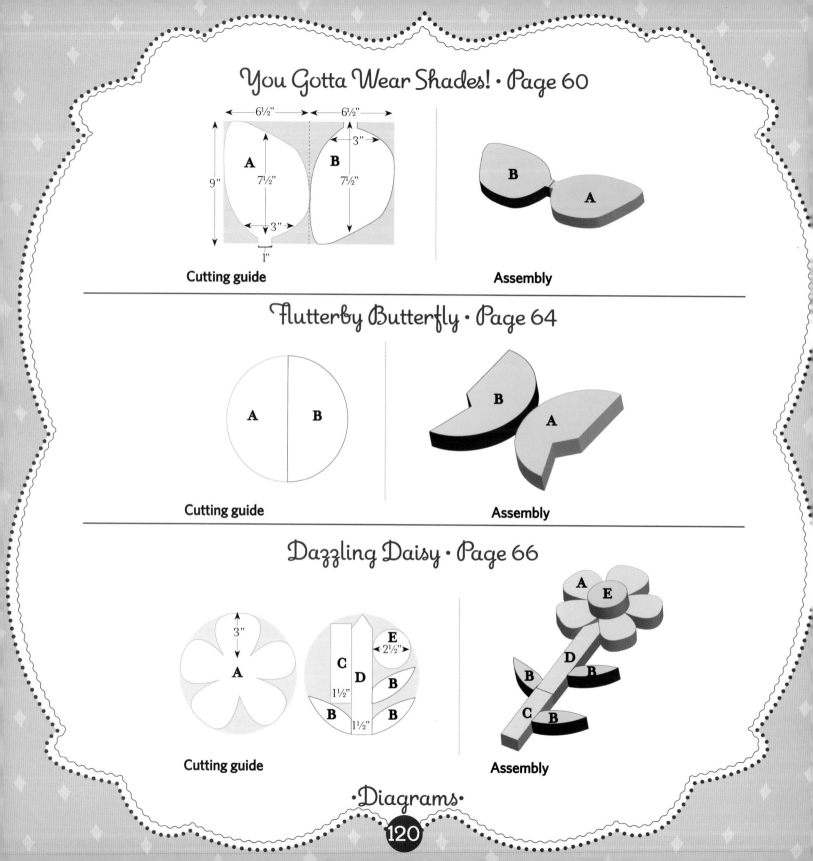

Cutting guide

Assembly

Flutterby Butterfly · Page 64

Cutting guide

Assembly

Dazzling Daisy · Page 66

Cutting guide

Assembly

·Diagrams·

Smiling Snail · Page 70

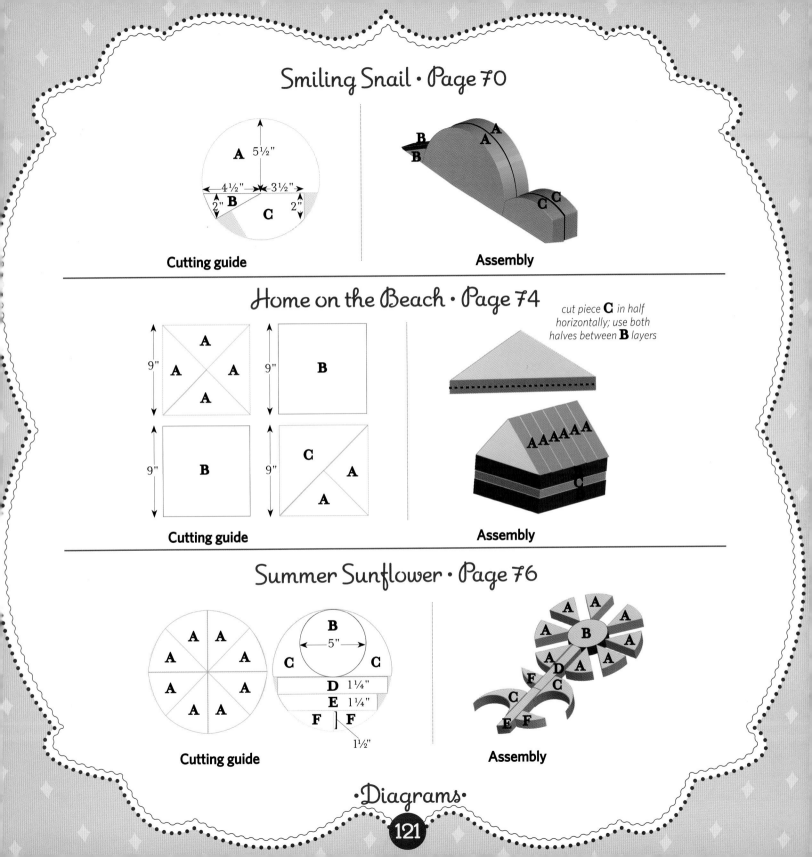

Cutting guide

A 5½"

4½"   3½"

2" **B**   **C**   2"

Assembly

Home on the Beach · Page 74

*cut piece **C** in half horizontally; use both halves between **B** layers*

Cutting guide

9"   **A**   A A A

9"   **B**

9"   **B**

9"   C A A

Assembly

A A A A A A

C

Summer Sunflower · Page 76

Cutting guide

A A A A A A A A

B 5"

C   C

D 1¼"

E 1¼"

F   F

1½"

Assembly

A A A
A B A
A D A
F A
C
E F

Charming Thatched Cottage · Page 80

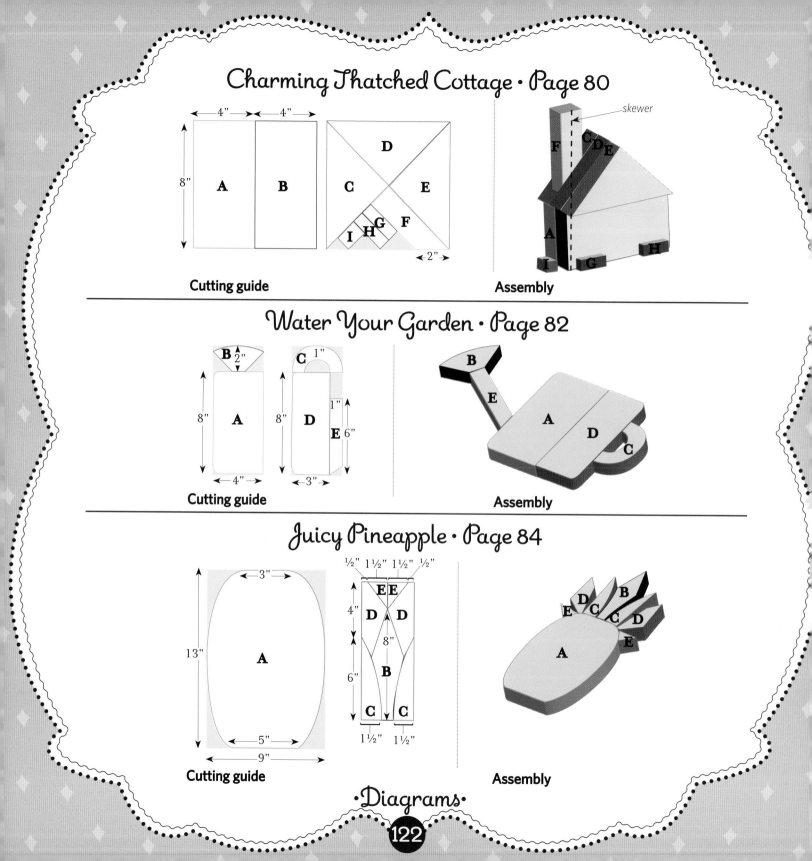

4"   4"

8"

A   B

D

C   E

I H G F

←2"→

skewer

F   C D E

A

I   G   H

Cutting guide

Assembly

Water Your Garden · Page 82

B 2"

C 1"

8"

A

8"

D

1"

E 6"

4"

3"

B

E

A

D

C

Cutting guide

Assembly

Juicy Pineapple · Page 84

3"

13"

A

5"

9"

½" 1½" 1½" ½"

E E

4"

D   D

8"

B

6"

C   C

1½" 1½"

D   B

E   C   C   D

E

A

Cutting guide

Assembly

·Diagrams·

The Chef's Special · Page 92

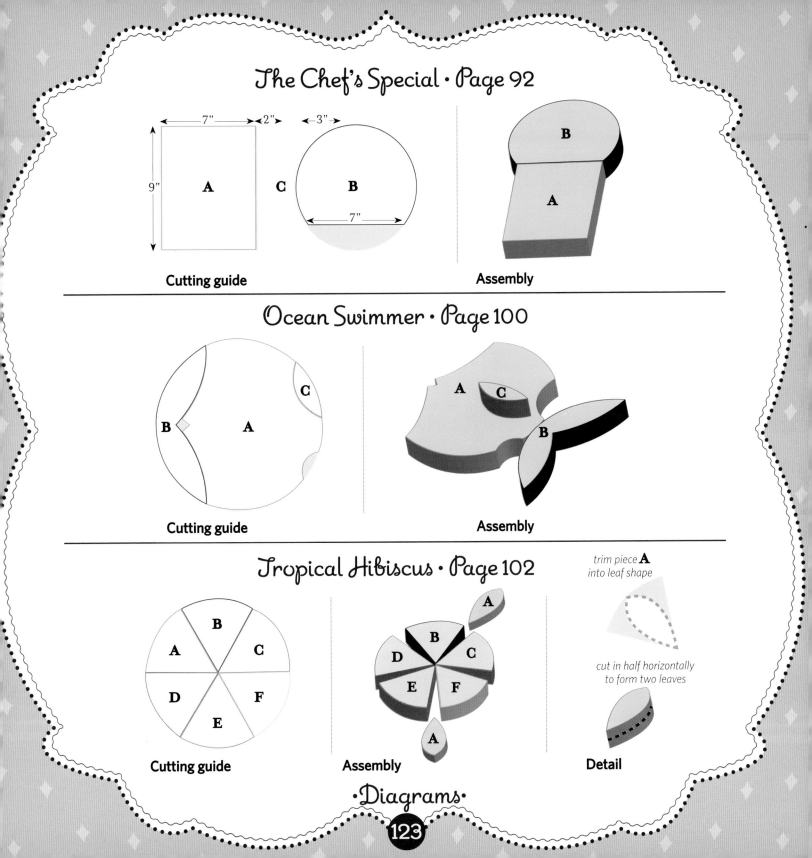

| 7" | 2" | 3" |
| 9" | | 7" |

A **C** **B**

Cutting guide

B **A**

Assembly

Ocean Swimmer · Page 100

C

B **A**

Cutting guide

A **C**

B

Assembly

Tropical Hibiscus · Page 102

*trim piece **A** into leaf shape*

B

A **C**

D **F**

E

Cutting guide

A

B

D **C**

E **F**

A

Assembly

cut in half horizontally to form two leaves

Detail

Crabby Crustacean · Page 104

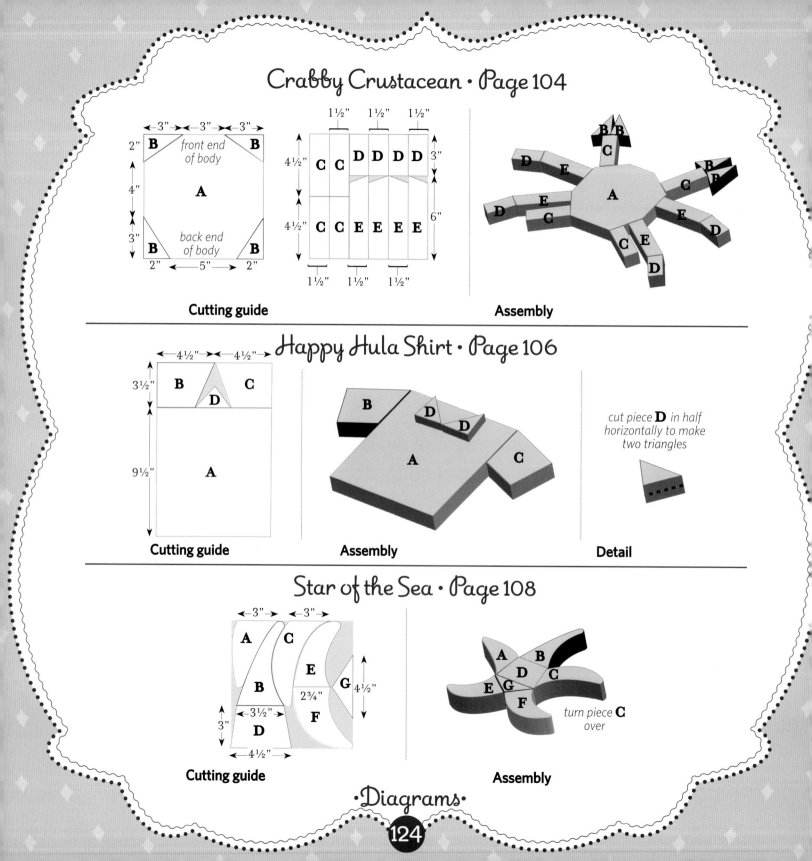

B front end of body **B**

3" 3" 3"

2"

A

4"

3"

B back end of body **B**

2" 5" 2"

Cutting guide

1½" 1½" 1½"

4½"

C **C** **D** **D** **D** **D**

3"

4½"

C **C** **E** **E** **E** **E**

6"

1½" 1½" 1½"

Assembly

Happy Hula Shirt · Page 106

4½" 4½"

3½"

B **C**

D

9½"

A

Cutting guide

Assembly

B **D** **D** **A** **C**

*cut piece **D** in half horizontally to make two triangles*

Detail

Star of the Sea · Page 108

3" 3"

A **C**

B **E** **G**

4½"

3½"

2¾"

3"

D **F**

4½"

Cutting guide

A **B** **D** **E** **G** **C** **F**

*turn piece **C** over*

Assembly

·Diagrams·

Underwater View · Page 110

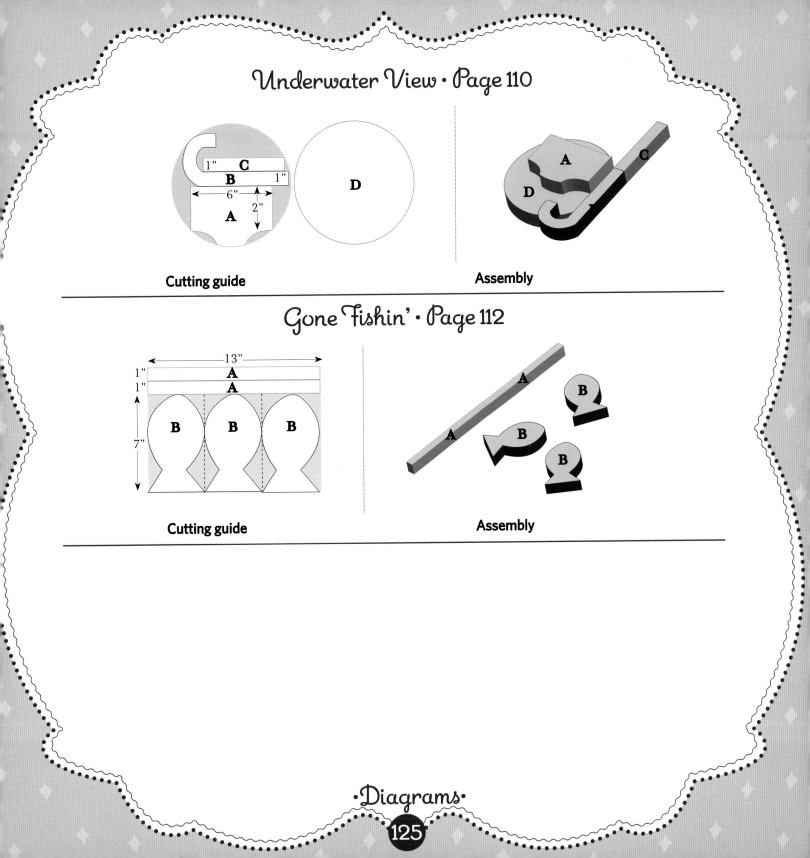

Cutting guide

Assembly

Gone Fishin' · Page 112

Cutting guide

Assembly

·Fun with Cake Scraps·

What can you do with all those leftover cake scraps? It's tempting to munch on the trimmings from your cakes as you cut them into pieces, but there are better—and even more delicious—uses for these bits of leftover cake.

Freeze the scraps in heavy-duty freezer bags and turn them into tasty treats for your family and friends. The simplest way to use up cake scraps is in a trifle: Cut the frozen cake pieces into small chunks and layer them in parfait glasses with fresh fruit, yogurt or pudding.

Fondues are a fun and easy way to enjoy cake scraps, especially if you have extra pound cake. Melt one 12-ounce package of semisweet or bittersweet chocolate chips with ⅓ cup whipping cream and serve with cake cubes and fruit for dipping.

Cake bonbons are another good way to use up both leftover cake scraps and frosting. Try different flavor combinations, or add a little peanut butter or jam to the basic recipe for a change of pace. The possibilities are endless!

Cake Bonbons

4 cups lightly packed fresh cake crumbs*
¼ cup frosting
1½ to 3 teaspoons flavored coffee creamer or liqueur
2 bars (4 ounces each) bittersweet chocolate, chopped

*Crumble cake scraps until they resemble coarse crumbs.

1. Combine cake crumbs, frosting and 1½ teaspoons creamer in medium bowl; gently mix until evenly blended. If mixture seems dry, add more creamer, 1 teaspoon at a time.

2. Form mixture into 1-inch balls, rolling between palms until evenly shaped. Place on waxed paper-lined baking sheet; refrigerate until ready to use.

3. Place chocolate in glass measuring cup; microwave on MEDIUM (50% power) 60 to 90 seconds. Stir; microwave in 30-second intervals until chocolate is melted and smooth.

4. Place cake ball on skewer and dip into melted chocolate, covering completely. Tap skewer gently to let excess chocolate drip back into cup. Place coated cake ball on waxed paper. Repeat with remaining cake balls, reheating chocolate on MEDIUM, if necessary. Let stand until chocolate sets.   *Makes 32 to 36 bonbons*

Variations: Roll balls of cake mixture in cocoa powder, powdered sugar, finely chopped nuts, colored sprinkles or finely crushed cookie crumbs.

• Index •

METRIC CONVERSION CHART

VOLUME MEASUREMENTS (dry)

1/8 teaspoon = 0.5 mL
1/4 teaspoon = 1 mL
1/2 teaspoon = 2 mL
3/4 teaspoon = 4 mL
1 teaspoon = 5 mL
1 tablespoon = 15 mL
2 tablespoons = 30 mL
1/4 cup = 60 mL
1/3 cup = 75 mL
1/2 cup = 125 mL
2/3 cup = 150 mL
3/4 cup = 175 mL
1 cup = 250 mL
2 cups = 1 pint = 500 mL
3 cups = 750 mL
4 cups = 1 quart = 1 L

VOLUME MEASUREMENTS (fluid)

1 fluid ounce (2 tablespoons) = 30 mL
4 fluid ounces (1/2 cup) = 125 mL
8 fluid ounces (1 cup) = 250 mL
12 fluid ounces (1 1/2 cups) = 375 mL
16 fluid ounces (2 cups) = 500 mL

WEIGHTS (mass)

1/2 ounce = 15 g
1 ounce = 30 g
3 ounces = 90 g
4 ounces = 120 g
8 ounces = 225 g
10 ounces = 285 g
12 ounces = 360 g
16 ounces = 1 pound = 450 g

DIMENSIONS

1/16 inch = 2 mm
1/8 inch = 3 mm
1/4 inch = 6 mm
1/2 inch = 1.5 cm
3/4 inch = 2 cm
1 inch = 2.5 cm

OVEN TEMPERATURES

250°F = 120°C
275°F = 140°C
300°F = 150°C
325°F = 160°C
350°F = 180°C
375°F = 190°C
400°F = 200°C
425°F = 220°C
450°F = 230°C

BAKING PAN SIZES

Utensil	Size in Inches/Quarts	Metric Volume	Size in Centimeters
Baking or Cake Pan (square or rectangular)	8 × 8 × 2	2 L	20 × 20 × 5
	9 × 9 × 2	2.5 L	23 × 23 × 5
	12 × 8 × 2	3 L	30 × 20 × 5
	13 × 9 × 2	3.5 L	33 × 23 × 5
Loaf Pan	8 × 4 × 3	1.5 L	20 × 10 × 7
	9 × 5 × 3	2 L	23 × 13 × 7
Round Layer Cake Pan	8 × 1½	1.2 L	20 × 4
	9 × 1½	1.5 L	23 × 4
Pie Plate	8 × 1¼	750 mL	20 × 3
	9 × 1¼	1 L	23 × 3
Baking Dish or Casserole	1 quart	1 L	—
	1½ quart	1.5 L	—
	2 quart	2 L	—